Mountain Prayers

RACINE, WI

Mountain Prayers: A Vacation for Your Soul
ISBN: 978-1-970103-30-4 - *Paperback*
ISBN: 978-1-970103-31-1 - *Hardcover*
ISBN: 978-1-970103-54-0 - *Ebook*
Copyright © 2022 Honor Books
Racine, WI

Cover Design by Faille Schmitz. Manuscript written and compiled by Rebecca Currington, Vicki J. Kuyper, Patricia Mitchell, and Julie Sutton in association with Snapdragon Group Editorial Services.

Introduction

Vacation means time away. Time for rest, renewal, a break from responsibility. Time to settle back and realign your physical, mental, emotional, and spiritual center of gravity. No wonder so many people choose to spend their vacations in the mountains, where rivers, forests, peaks, and valleys combine to elevate the soul. It's natural!

Mountain Prayers: A Vacation for Your Soul was written expressly to inspire your vacation, whether you're reading from the comfort of your living room sofa or sitting on a boulder after cresting a ridge. You'll find fascinating meditations on life, encouragement from God's Word, inspiring quotes, and heartfelt prayers to put everything in perspective. We hope this unpretentious volume will give you the friendly little push you need to make these insights real in your life.

It's going to be a wonderful, restful time. God bless you as you read, relax, and just "be."

I will refresh the weary and satisfy the faint.
JEREMIAH 31:25

Climbing Higher

---

*I have fought a good fight, I have finished my
course, I have kept the faith.*
2 TIMOTHY 4:7 KJV

You line up with a crew of hikers at the base of Mount Everest. Your group looks like ants in comparison to the mammoth mountain before you. Yet with heavy backpacks strapped over your shoulders, hiking boots covering your feet, and determination in your mind, you head up the long windy trail single file. With the wind at your face, the sun at your back, and a light fog surrounding you. you climb the rocky path.

You and your group rest only for a short time. After consuming energy bars and much needed water, up you go. Every muscle in your body is put to the grueling test as you continue up the side of the steep ravine. You know that daytime hours are limited and you must move on in order to reach your goal. When night falls you try to find a flat section away from the mountain's edge. Unloading your packs, you build a fire, pitch a tent, and settle in for a much needed sleep.

Before sunrise you awake, pack up your gear, and set out. You face many dangers along the way. Sometimes the slopes are slippery and paved with ice. Sometimes the way is rocky and covered in loose gravel. Sometimes the winds are so violent your pace is slowed to a crawl. In spite of all the dangers Mother Nature hurls at you, you are determined to reach the summit.

It's the same with us in our Christian walk. There are many dangers around us. There are many obstacles that slow us down or try to get in our way. However, just like an avid mountain climber, we have to focus on our goal: reaching the summit.

What mountains are you facing? Why not give them to Jesus? For it is only when we climb higher with God, and trust him to take us to the next level, that we ultimately achieve our goals.

For our light and momentary troubles are
achieving for us an eternal glory that far
outweighs them all.
2 CORINTHIANS 4:17

Heavenly Father:

The mountains before me are imposing, but I will not fear. I know that you are able to help me achieve the goals set before me. Thank you for your helping hand along the upward trail — for that bit of extra strength, that sudden insight when the path is uncertain, that infusion of determination when I become tired and discouraged.

Amen.

Spring Thaw

Let us acknowledge the Lord; let us press on to acknowledge him. As surely as the sun rises, he will appear: he will come to us like the winter rains, like the spring rains that water the earth.

HOSEA 6:3

You gaze out at the snowcapped mountains and feel the warm sun on your skin. Spring rains kiss your flower garden. Birds flock in pairs, fluttering, chirping merrily as they gather twigs. Trees burst forth with new life. The fresh smell of flowers penetrates your stuffy nose. You can't help but be taken in by the beauty of spring. You love retreating to the cabin just as the deep freeze begins to thaw.

Although this is a normal part of the cycle of life, and it's magnificent to watch, adverse effects often occur. Melting snow along with heavy rains can produce flash floods, washed-out roads, and flooded homes that leave whole towns in disarray. It can't be helped. Sometimes even the most beautiful things can have adverse effects. Just like spring, adversity is part of life. You can count on it!

What adversity or hardship are you facing in your life? Hopefully it's not as devastating as a flood caused by melting snow. But even if it is, you won't have to face it alone. God promises to be there with you to enjoy the spring thaw in whatever area of life it comes—physical, emotional, mental, or spiritual—and help you face any of the adverse effects you might encounter in the process. He know's that even the floods leave fertile soil behind, enriching your life and decorating it with beautiful springtime flowers.

So drag a chair out onto the deck, have a seat, and take it all in. Listen and enjoy as the spring thaw comes to your cabin and to your heart. It's magnificent!

Rejoice in the Lord your God, for he has given you the autumn rains in righteousness. He sends you abundant showers, both autumn and spring rains, as before. The threshing floors will be filled with grain, the vats will overflow with new wine and oil.
JOEL 2:23-24

Adversity is like the period of the rain . . . cold, comfortless, unfriendly to man and to animal; yet from that season have their birth the flower, the fruit, the date, the rose, and the pomegranate.
SIR WALTER SCOTT

Dear Lord:

Thank you for bringing a spring thaw to my frozen heart. I welcome the rains as they mingle with the melting snow. I know they will bring beauty and renewal to my life.

Amen.

Washed Away

Wash me thoroughly from my iniquity,
and cleanse me from my sin.
PSALM 51: 1-2 NRSV

A steady pitter pat of raindrops keeps rhythm on your roof. The gentle rain falls from heaven, saturating everything around your cottage. You peer out the bay window overlooking the water. The sun is hidden behind the clouds. Yesterday's footprints are gone. The dirt on the patio is washed away.

You notice how everything looks so fresh and clean after a good rain. The trees are fuller. The grass greener. The sky bluer. The sun brighter.

You step outside and breathe in that mountain air. Fresh. Clean. Exhilarating. Amazing what one little shower can do, isn't it?

Rain is one of the ways the earth cleans itself. We'd have to scrub for hours to do what rain can do in just a few minutes. Rainwater is a natural purifier to all vegetation. It also facilitates growth. Without it, the world as we know it today would be dead.

When there's not enough rain, drought sets in. The ground dries up. Plants shrivel. Streams disappear, liven healthy drinking water becomes rare. However there is an even worse drought—the drought you can go through spiritually. Your devotion time becomes dry, stagnant. It seems as though you're just going through the motions. You want to be full, but you're empty. You need some water—some living water.

Jesus came to wash all sin away, to make atonement for us. to fill us to overflowing, so we'd never thirst again. Take a few' moments to bask in God's presence, thank him for his cleansing power, trust him to fill you, and ask him to wash all the impurities away like a refreshing mountain rain.

For you know that it was not with perishable things such as silver or gold that you were redeemed from the empty way of life handed down to you from your forefathers, but with the precious blood of Christ, a lamb without blemish or defect.
1 PETER 1:18-19

Jesus accepts you the way you are, but loves you too much to leave you that way.
LEE VENDEN

Dear Lord:

I want and need your cleansing rain. Let it pour over my life, washing away all those attitudes, behaviors, and thoughts that keep me from having a full, open, confident relationship with you. Thank you for your love that paid the price for my sins and made the rain of forgiveness possible.

Amen.

An Attitude of Gratitude

Be made new in the attitude of your minds.
EPHESIANS 4:23

You glance outside with distaste. It's a dreary day. You'd hoped for sunshine, a trip down the river rapids on a raft, some fishing, and a nice dinner cooked over an open fire. Instead the weather man rules. Nothing today but torrential rains.

You may feel like the day is ruined—but don't be so quick to dismiss your hope for a great time. You can't control the weather, but you can control your attitude. How you react is up to you. You have a choice. It may not be shooting the rapids and cooking out as you had anticipated, but if you're looking, you'll find that there are many memorable things to do on a mountain vacation.

Stop for a moment and look around you. Your rented cabin is a pleasant refuge from the storms outside. This might be the perfect day for resting—an essential part of any vacation. Read a book, spend some time in prayer, take five naps—in a row!

The point of course is that belaboring what isn't happening often causes us to miss out on the great things that could be happening. That's clearly a waste of your precious vacation time, but nothing that can't be redeemed with a little attitude adjustment.

Even when things don't go your way, you have so much to be grateful for—like the fact that God loves you and has made you an heir to his promises. In life, as on vacation, there are no guarantees. Adversity visits regularly whether you're in a lovely mountain cabin or walking through the everyday realities of your life. Greet it with an attitude that keeps you in the driver's seat. When the world gives you lemons, make lemonade. Hidden in that annoying cliche is a bit of spiritual truth. Life is as good as you decide to make it. Attitude, attitude, attitude.

Since then, you have been raised with Christ, set your hearts on things above, where Christ is seated at the right hand of God. Set your minds on things above, not on earthly things.
COLOSSIANS 3:1-2

The greatest part of our happiness depends on our dispositions, not our circumstances.
MARTHA WASHINGTON

Heavenly Father:

I'm so glad to have you in my life, and yet, I often mope around discouraged by petty problems rather than counting my blessings and exhibiting an attitude of gratitude. When I get to looking down rather than up, give me a nudge. Remind me of all I have to be thankful for.

Amen.

Balancing Act

This is what the Lord Almighty says:
"Give careful thought to your ways. "
HAGGAI 1:5

You walked what seemed like a hundred miles yesterday. How could you not? You saw so many wonderful things — sweet noble flowers growing from the crevices of rocks, mountain paths almost hidden from view, even an enormous bird's nest, which you observed from a safe distance. The first day of vacation and you wanted to see everything at once. Now all you can bear to do is slip into the hot tub — hoping for some relief. Every muscle in your body aches. Even places you didn't know' you had muscles hurt. The thought crosses your mind that even good things need to be done in moderation.

It's good to be moderate in all aspects of your life — on vacation and back home in the hectic activities of your daily routine. When you get yourself going in too many directions, trying to accomplish too much too fast, you may find yourself wracked with aches and pains as well — the kind that leave you feeling overwhelmed, exhausted, and sick.

God has no interest in spoiling your fun, but he does want to see you live a happy, energetic, healthy, and well-balanced life. He knows that when you do, you will be able to achieve all the things he's planned for you.

Right now while you're resting there in the hot tub letting your muscles relax and the aches and pains melt away, resolve to do things differently when you get back home. Set your mind to live as God would have you to live, a solid life filled with equal parts of work and fun, solitude, and fellowship.

Everything should be done in a fitting and
orderly way.
1 CORINTHIANS 14:40

"Holy leisure" refers to a sense of balance in the
life, an ability to be at peace though the activities
of the day, an ability to rest and take time to
enjoy beauty, an ability to pace ourselves.
RICHARD J. FOSTER

Heavenly Father:

I live in extremes: too much work, too much solitude, too much striving toward the goal, not enough time resting. Help me to find a proper balance for my life. I know that begins in the little things. When I feel that pull to work just a few more hours, push just a little harder, do just one more thing, remind me that there will be a price to pay. Thanks for helping me do my best without missing out on your best for me.

Amen.

Under the Waterfall

Do not let this Book of the Law depart from your mouth: meditate on it day and night, so that you may be careful to do everything written in it. Then you will be prosperous and successful.
JOSHUA 1:8

You've heard about the beauty of mountains. Now you see it face to face. The green slopes, the vast fields of w'ildflow'ers. the multiplying wildlife, and especially the breathtaking waterfalls. You stand in awe as you Watch the water flow out of a nearby cliff and splash down on the rocks below.

Have you noticed how everything connected to this waterfall, even the river below, is alive and flowing with new life? In a sense, that waterfall is more than a gorgeous example of God's creative genius. It also provides a source of nutrition and life to creatures and wildlife in the depths and valleys of the earth.

That's what the Bible does for you too. It's a powerful source of God's rich nutrients being sent down from heaven. You can sit and soak it all in like a deer who's been thirsting for water, grateful for a refreshing drink.

God doesn't want you to run dry. He wants to fill you full. He wants to pour into you every good and perfect thing. But he cannot force you to drink. He has gone to great lengths to make sure that is your choice. You must decide to open your mind and your heart and take it in.

Perhaps it's been awhile since you felt full. It may have even been awhile since you really have just sat down and absorbed all that God has for you both in his Word and in life. Take some time today to come to the waterfall of God's Word. Be cleansed. Be filled. Be renewed.

The law of the Lord is perfect, reviving the soul.
The statutes of the Lord are trustworthy, making
wise the simple.
P S A L M   1 9 : 7

By reading the Scriptures I am so renewed that
all nature seems renewed around me and with
me. The sky seems to be a pure, a cooler blue, the
trees a deeper green.
T H O M A S   M E R T O N

Dear Lord:

Thank you for the cool, refreshing waters of your Word. As I lose
myself in its pages, bring renewal to my parched soul, replace my
emptiness with living water. Without your Word I would wither
and die, never to be what you created me to be. But when I apply it
to my life, nothing is impossible.

Amen.

A Blessing in Disguise

We know that all things work together for good
for those who love God.
ROMANS 8:2.8 NRSV

Out for a walk in the mountain air, you watch a bee land atop a budding wildflower. With tiny wings vibrating, it buzzes and flutters in your direction. You take a step back, remembering the last time you were stung.

Although bee stings aren't pleasant, you might say bees are a blessing in disguise. They pollinate your flowers and make your garden look beautiful. Though they make you uncomfortable, even frighten you, you wouldn't want to do away with them entirely. You put up with them, understanding that their presence benefits you.

Bee stings and pain are alike in that way — pain can also be a blessing in disguise. Months of discomfort and hours of labor come before that newborn baby. Uncomfortable, even sickening, regimens of chemotherapy come before remission. And often years of struggle and hard work lead up to that day when you settle in to a well-earned retirement with money enough to see you through.

All blessings — all disguised.

Maybe you should take a good, hard look at the unpleasant aspects of your life. Despite the discomfort they are causing you, can you see that lessons are being learned, character is being built, your faith is being strengthened? Is there purpose in your pain?

The Lord promises in the Bible that he will turn every situation, every circumstance, every moment of suffering into something good for our lives. Somewhere in it all there will be a silver lining, something important and beneficial.

Remember the lesson of the bee buzzing around the mountainside, sometimes causing pain but always bringing life and beauty. When you do, your troubles will take on new meaning.

> *What a stack of blessing you have piled up for*
> *those who worship you. Ready and waiting for*
> *all who run to you to escape an unkind world.*
> *PSALM 31:19 MSG*

> *Lift up your eyes, the heavenly Father waits to*
> *bless you - in inconceivable ways to make your*
> *life what you never dreamed it could be.*
> *ANNE ORTLUND*

Precious Lord:

How can I ever thank you for all the blessings you have poured out on me — some straightforward and others in disguise. I am grateful for your goodness, your unearned generosity, your unexplainable kindnesses to me. You are a great and wonderful God!

Amen.

Change Sets Us Free

Therefore, if anyone is in Christ, he is a new creation, the old has gone, the new has come!
2 CORINTHIANS 5:17

Snowcapped mountains begin to thaw. The brown grass turns green. The gray skies turn a bright shade of blue. Dead flowers come to life bursting with new blossoms. A monarch butterfly takes flight before your eyes. The sun kisses your face, warming your red, chilly nose. It's all part of the marvelous change from winter to spring. And it's all happening right before your eyes as you watch from the deck of your cabin.

Makes you think, doesn't it, about all the changes in your own life. Changes in plans, desires, hopes, dreams. Moves from one place to another, one season of life to another. The interesting thing is that you always thought of those changes as being negative, but that doesn't jive with what you are seeing right now in this place. These changes are good, productive, beneficial. They signal that the earth is moving, renewing itself. How unpleasant and yes, even perilous, it would be if winter never ended—365 days of snow and ice and bitter cold. For that matter, it wouldn't be much better to be trapped in summer, spring, or fall. The changing of the seasons is a gift from God—and so are the changes you've experienced. Each one has added complexity and depth to your life.

Spiritual change is also good. The Bible warns about simply receiving God's gift of salvation and then settling in, never growing in the faith, never getting to know God better, never coming to a full realization of all your heavenly Father has planned for you.

As you sit there on the deck, sipping your coffee and drawing the fresh mountain air into your lungs, ask yourself if you have really embraced change in the way God intended. The process is sometimes painful, but it's good pain. Even though you are leaving some things behind, you are also moving in the direction of greater things yet to come. That's what being alive is all about.

Praise be to the name of God for ever and ever, wisdom and power are his. He changes times and seasons, he sets up kings and deposes them. He gives wisdom to the wise and knowledge to the discerning. He reveals deep and hidden things; he knows what lies in darkness, and light dwells with him.
DANIEL 2:20-22

Who would be constant in happiness must often change.
CHINESE PROVERB

Dear Lord:

I know I fight change. I want to cling to the familiar, the comfortable. Forgive me for my reticence to step forward into all you have prepared for me. Give me the courage to embrace change and all its many benefits.

Amen.

A Sweet Choice

Without good direction, people lose their way:
the more wise counsel you follow, the better your
chances.
PROVERBS 44:14 MSG

You flip through tons of brochures. A mountain resort with lots of skiing sounds good. But you also want to take that helicopter ride, visit the aquarium, and get together with friends you haven't chatted with in a while.

You face dozens of choices each day. They may be as trivial as what toothpaste is best to whiten your teeth, or which shampoo is right for dry hair. Or maybe even how or with whom you will spend your vacation.

Choices can also be more complex — like what man or woman you'll choose to date, who you'll marry, or even how many kids you'll have. The results of those choices affects not only your moods and your physical life but also your spiritual life. Your choices can bring you closer to God or push you away from him.

You may not know it. but God has provided a road map to help you make wise, informed choices. The Bible contains "righteous principles" that are designed to help you navigate a dangerous world. When heeded they will help you see clearly even in the fog of cultural relativism and humanistic babble.

In addition to the Bible, God invites you to come to him in prayer and ask for help. When you do, he's promised to give you the wisdom you need to find the right path. God has also promised to speak to your heart. Making the right choices in this world isn't easy, but God has given you the tools you will need to stay on track.

You don't have to waste precious life hours belaboring your choices. God has given you wonderful resources to help you. That will make your choices sweet!

Preserve sound judgment and discernment, do not let them out of your sight: they will be life for you. an ornament to grace your neck. Then you will go on your way in safety, and your foot will not stumble: when you lie down, you will not be afraid when you lie down, your sleep will be sweet.
PROVERBS 3:21-24

God gives man a will,
but he must make the right choices.
FULTON J. SHEEN

Dear Father:

I know that you have given me everything I need to make good choices for my life – if only I would heed your provisions. Forgive me when I fail to listen, when I do my own thing and then wonder why I've got a mess later. Thank you for helping me make good choices in the future.

Amen.

Rise Up with Wings as Eagles

This is what the Lord says to you: "Do not be
afraid or discouraged . . . For the battle is not
yours, but God's."
1 CHRONICLES 20:15

I t's storming outside. You pull the drapes and peer through the glass balcony doors and notice an eagle. Graceful and peaceful, yet also courageous, he soars through the stormy sky. Unlike most birds, the eagle doesn't seem concerned with the rain or even the thunder and lightning. Instead of taking shelter, he goes higher. After awhile, he disappears.

You assume he's probably flown back to his nest, but that's not the case. Eagles actually have the ability to rise above the clouds. In the face of challenges, they are unflappable, meeting every situation head on.

Eagles are remarkable in other ways as well. For example, they are the only birds that can fly straight into the sun, and they can catch fish that weigh twice as much as they do. One of their secrets is to thoroughly clean every section of their wings. As they breathe on each feather, an oil is produced that protects them from sun, wind, and water. Perhaps this is the reason for their courage and confidence.

You may be facing a challenge right now. Perhaps you can't seem to evade your fears. They pursue you wherever you go—even on vacation. Maybe you are carrying a heavy load—some burden that is weighing you down. Or you may find yourself in the midst of a storm of circumstances. Whatever the situation, God will be with you. He will not let your fears overwhelm you. Nor will he allow you to drown or be swallowed up in rain, wind, and lightning. Just as the eagle rises in confidence and courage, so will you.

Next time you're facing a challenge, instead of cowering in the shadows, think of the eagle. Take the time to prepare like the eagle does when it cleanses its wings. This is done through Bible reading and prayer. Then look into the Son, take a leap of faith, and let God take you above the storms in your life. You'll experience a courage you've never known.

I am the Lord, your God, who takes hold of your right hand and says to you, "Do not fear, I will help you."
ISAIAH 41:13

Courage is fear that has said its prayers.
DOROTHY BERNARD

Heavenly Father:

Help me to face the challenges in my life with faith and courage, looking to you to help me gain authority over my fears. Show me how to soar high above the troubles in my life, remembering that you will never fail me. Thank you for keeping me in all my ways, just as you do the eagle.

Amen.

27

Sheltering Tree

The eternal God is your refuge, and underneath
are the everlasting arms.
DEUTERONOMY 33:27

From your perch on the side of the mountain, look up into the trees, and you're sure to spot birds' nests nestled in the branches. Though the nests appear fragile, they're actually tightly woven and weather sturdy, able to protect their tiny occupants from drenching rains and damaging winds. So securely placed are the nests that when branches bend and sway, the nests hold firm. How marvelous is God, who gave even the birds of the forests and woodlands a way to protect themselves and their young from storms!

The same Creator God is even more concerned about you. He invites you to "build a nest" in the strong tree of his Word so you can withstand the storms and stresses of life. In his Word, he reveals to you his commandments to protect you from harmful decisions and actions. He reveals to you the Good News of Jesus Christ to protect you from the ravages of despair and hopelessness. He gives you his Holy Spirit to plant, nurture, and strengthen your faith, a faith tightly woven and weather sturdy, a faith to withstand the storms of life.

On mountain hikes, you've seen a fallen branch or noticed a nest destroyed and abandoned on the ground. Yes, the trees of the forest sometimes fail, as anything or anyone on this earth might. That's why God wants you to rely on nothing less than his protection, because he will never fail. Though everything else falls around you. you will remain standing in the stronghold in his Word—your sheltering tree. How marvelous is God—your God—who holds you in safety and security!

Look for a little nest snuggled high in the branches. Then praise your God forgiving you a place in the sheltering tree of his protective care.

If you make the Most High your dwelling —
even the Lord, who is my refuge — then no harm
will befall you, no disaster will come near your
tent. For he will command his angels concerning
you to guard you in all your ways.
PSALM 91:9-11

Safe am I, safe am I in the hollow of His hand.
MILDRED LEIGHTNER DILLON

Dear Lord:

Thank you for providing uncompromised protection for me in the storms of life. I realize that this does not mean that a storm will never blow my way — only that you will sustain me as it passes through my life. I'm so grateful for your loving care.

Amen.

Next Steps

*Both high and low among men find refuge in the
shadow of your wings. They feast on the
abundance of your house; you give them drink
from your river of delights.*

P S A L M   3 6 : 7 - 8

A woman, beset with worries about her future, came to this very mountain cabin for a few weeks of rest and reflection. The career she had followed for decades appeared to be ending, and she needed direction. It was during this time that she noticed the pine needles covering the ground. She picked up a few and rolled them with her fingers. Slowly, she began to work with them. Now she owns a thriving business in handcrafted pine baskets, bowls, containers, and jewelry.

God provides. Yes, sometimes he provides by means of a stunning miracle, but most often he provides by means of the quiet blessings right around you. Gathering and using his provisions becomes a matter of attentiveness. Day-to-day attentiveness opens your eyes to the countless ways God opens his hands to you.

Imagine a bird's-eye view of the mountain range. Awe-inspiring for sure, but not the same as standing where you are now, with your feet on the ground, able to see and touch one tree. In the shades of green, the textured bark, and the fragrance of pine you take in the wonder of God's creation, up close and personal. Likewise with attentiveness. The more attention you pay to the people, events, and circumstances right around you, the more you become aware of the many quiet blessings God puts in your path every day. He provides ways for you to grow closer to him and grow in faith. Ways for you to serve him and others in the things you do and say. Ways for you to gather and use his provisions to the fullest.

As you spend time in the mountains looking out at the trees and sky, listening to the call of birds and the chattering of squirrels in the morning, and feeling the soft warmth of the evening's campfire at night, give God the same kind of mindful attention. His provisions are all around you—perhaps right at your feet!

[God] has shown kindness by giving you rain from heaven and crops in their seasons; he provides you with plenty of food and fills your hearts with joy.
A C T S   1 4 : 1 7

There is no need too great for God. He has unlimited resources at His disposal, and He delights in making them available to His children.
M E R I W E T H E R   W I L L I A M S

Dear Father:

I thank you for your abundant provision in my life. When I needed wisdom, you gave it. When I needed hope, you sent it my way. When I had material needs, you found a way to meet them. I can count on you — always — and that's a wonderful thing.

Amen.

A Timely Plan

There is a time for everything, and a season for
every activity under heaven.
E C C L E S I A S T E S   3 : 4

"In America," according to a German proverb, "an hour is forty minutes." Yes, Americans go for speed, convenience, and a rapid response to their needs and demands. You easily forget about that forty-minute hour, however, as you hike among centuries-old trees in the timeless majesty of the mountains. You savor the morning's chirp and chatter of forest life and the fragrance of dew-draped earth . . . the gurgle of a hidden creek and the slant of the sun's rays across your path as the afternoon's shadows gently wrap you in evening's peace. Nature knows no forty-minute hour. Its times, its seasons, take place according to God's divine plan for his creation.

Before the world began, God had a plan for your life. Before you were born, God prepared your hours and seasons, and he held in his hands your times of shadow and light, of challenge and success, of loss and renewal. Because he did, nothing happens to you out of its time. Neither need you worry that time is running away from you . . . or that time isn't on your side . . . or that you're out of time to do what he wants you to do or go where he wants you to go. Not when you're on God's timetable—and you are. According to his timing, you're right where he knew he would find you today.

When you wish time would hurry up, think again.

Consider what would happen if a butterfly left her cocoon in the middle of winter, or a blossom poked its head through frozen ground. Creation would shout, "Not yet! Not yet!" Everything you experience now is part of God's plan for you now. When he created the times of your life, he had his eye not on the moment, but on your eternal good.

[Jesus] said to them: "It is not for you to know the times or dates the Father has set by his own authority."
A C T S   1 : 7

Trust in God and you are never confounded in time or eternity.
DWIGHT L. MOODY

Heavenly Father:

I know I'm impatient, always wanting to be going and doing when instead I should be listening to your voice and trusting in your perfect timing for my life. I want to live as you intended, not a moment ahead or a moment behind. Help me, Lord, to rest in your wisdom each and every day.

Amen.

New Life

*"For surely I know the plans I have for you," says the
Lord, "Plans for your welfare and not for harm, to
give you a future with hope."*
JEREMIAH 29:11 NRSV

Mountain forest fires cause massive loss, sometimes reducing to ashes hundreds of acres of trees, shrubs, and brush. Whether ignited by a streak of lightning or a spark from a campfire, forest fires leave charred hills, abandoned habitat, and mountainsides ripe for mudslides — a stark testament to fire's destructive power.

On assessing the after-effects of a forest fire, you might sigh, "It's God's will." Perhaps these same words came to mind the last time you looked over the bleak landscape of personal loss. To a point, the statement speaks the truth: nothing happens — forest fires, human pain — without God's knowledge and permission. But the words mislead you if you utter them with a sigh of resignation, concluding that God wills disappointment, destruction, or death. Though he allows it to happen in this fallen world, he doesn't will it. Instead, God controls the destructive events and painful circumstances sin brought into the world and turns them to serve his good and holy will. From the losses caused by a forest fire, he brings forth new life. Seeds of rebirth take root in cleared and fertile soil. Saplings sprout under bright sunshine, and forest animals return as the season changes, wild berries bloom and ripen, and streams find their way down the hills again. In the same way, God works in and through your hardships and losses, as well as your successes and celebrations, to achieve his perfect will.

Perhaps you can't see how anything good could possibly come out of the losses you have suffered. Possibly you'll be able to look back someday and recognize the rebirth happening in your life right now, or maybe you will never understand this side of heaven. But good will come, because God's will is good. That's why you and all God's people never mourn a loss without also giving thanks.

[Jesus said,] "My Father's will is that everyone who looks to the Son and believes in him shall have eternal life, and I will raise him up at the last day."
JOHN 6:40

There are no disappointments to those whose wills are buried in the will of God.
FREDERICK FABER

Dear Lord:

I know your will for my life includes only good things, for you are a kind and loving parent. Still I live in a world where suffering and loss are realities. Thank you for your promise that you will bring good even from my difficulties and disappointments. When my eyes are filled with tears. I will trust you to bring back my smile in due time according to your perfect will.

Amen.

The Voice of Authority

For everything that was written in the past was
written to teach us, so that through endurance
and the encouragement of the Scriptures we
might have hope.
ROMANS 15:4

When you were planning your vacation to the mountains, you paid attention to what travelers who had been there already had to say. It's unlikely you listened to the advice of people who have never left home, or based your expectations on someone's fantasies about mountains. You asked those who had been there and could speak with authority.

God's Word speaks with his authority through the lips of people who have "been there." The writer-witnesses truthfully reported what they had heard and seen. Prophets like Moses, Ezra, Isaiah, Amos, and Hosea proclaimed God's promises to his people, promises that came true in Jesus Christ. Apostles Matthew, John, and Peter followed Jesus during his ministry, witnessed his death, talked with him after his resurrection, then wrote the accounts you read today. Missionary Paul preached the gospel of Jesus' love for all people and saw the power of the gospel at work as the early church grew and spread throughout the known world. No writer of inspired Scripture wrote on the basis of hearsay or say-so or got away with weaving tales of creative fiction. The Bible is God's Word recorded by people who have been in relationship with him. They struggled with his commandments, questioned his will, tested his strength, and trusted him to keep his promises. But they also took God at his Word, relied on his strength, rejoiced in his healing, and found comfort in his peace.

On your spiritual journey, listen to those who have been there. Find out where you're headed, the best path to take, and what you'll find at your final destination. People who have "been there" speak in the Bible—God's authoritative Word for your travel.

The Bible is God's chart for you to steer by, to keep you from the bottom of the sea and to show you where the harbor is, and how to reach without running on rocks and bars.
HENRY WARD BEECHER

Dear Lord:

Thank you for your powerful Word filled with promises, life-giving principles, and the testimony of those who have trusted you and found you faithful. As I move through my life, I will read it often, learning from it what I need to know to make good choices and find right paths for my life.

Amen.

Heart and Lips

O give thanks to the Lord, call on his name,
make known bis deeds among the peoples.
Sing to him. sing praises to him,
tell of all his wonderful works.
1 *CHRONICLES 16:8-9 NRSV*

This morning you woke to the lilting songs of birds and chatter of chipmunks and squirrels. You felt the buttery glow of sunshine and took a deep breath of crisp, clean mountain air. Aaah! You found it easy to say, "Thank you, Lord. for the beginning of this great day!" But back home, when the alarm clock blares and you get out of bed to the glare of an electric light, "thank you" may come less easily. In fact, depending on what's ahead that day, it may not come at all.

The Bible says that you should say "thank you" every day — good days and bad days alike. You may feel that isn't a problem on the days when blessing seems to be plastered all over your life, but wonder why it's expected when misfortune comes your way — illness, financial troubles, problems in relationships, a setback at work. Why should you be grateful?

God's people are a thankful people because they have a constant expectation of good from a good God. No matter what they are facing on any given day, they know that deliverance, healing, consolation, encouragement, hope is on the way thanks to their faithful heavenly Father. When you say "Thank you, Lord," you are, by faith, showing confidence in what your wonderful, loving God is about to do on your behalf.

Wherever you are, whatever is happening in your life, begin to thank God for his mercy, his grace, and his lovingkindness. Thank him for all he's already done and for all he will do for you in the future. Establish a habit of gratitude. And when you're ready to pack up and go back home, don't forget to take your thankful heart—and lips—with you.

Praise the Lord! I will give thanks to the Lord
with my whole heart, in the company of the
upright, in the congregation.
Great are the works of the Lord,
studied by all who delight in them.
PSALM 111:1-2 NRSV

Gratitude to God makes even a temporal blessing
a taste of heaven.
WILLIAM ROMAINE

Dear Lord:

I am resolved to face every uncomfortable circumstance in my life
with a grateful heart. Thank you for your faithfulness to bring
good from every situation. You are a good and gracious heavenly
Father and I'm grateful, most of all, to be called your child.

Amen.

The Narrow Way

*Trust in the Lord with all your heart and lean
not on your own understanding; in all your
ways acknowledge him, and he will make your
paths straight.*

P R O V E R B S   3 : 5 - 6

Some hikers like to go off the beaten path and explore the mountainside for hidden streams and untouched coves. For others, a step off the marked trail will surely mean fear-filled hours of wandering lost in the forest. Whatever your hiking style, you should know that following Jesus will always take you off the beaten path.

Jesus called his way the narrow way. When you follow him. the crowd won't be going with you. Your principles and values, your priorities and ethics, your decisions and choices put you on the less-traveled path. But relax — there is no danger because he has promised to walk with you every step of the way. He accompanies you and guides you. Like a compass you carry in your backpack (especially if you venture into out-of-the-way places in the forest), Jesus points the direction as you travel. The Bible serves as a life map, giving guidance for ever)' possible eventuality. As you open your heart through prayer, he speaks to your heart, providing encouragement and affirmation. And it's simply impossible to get lost as long as you keep your hand in his.

Truthfully, the choice is yours. You can determine to stay in the safety and comfort of your mountain cabin, avoiding the hike altogether. Or you might choose to stick to the marked path, winding your way along with all the other hikers. But if you choose to leave the path and follow Jesus, you will be in for the adventure of a lifetime—one with eternal rewards. You will know the sweet closeness of his presence. You will feel his love and comfort. And you will know that your eternity is secure.

What will you choose—the beaten path or the path less traveled?

If I rise on the wings of the dawn, if I settle on the far side of the sea, even there your hand will guide me, your right hand will hold me fast.
PSALM 139:9 – 10

All the way my savior leads me; what have I to ask beside? Can I doubt His tender mercy, who through life had been my guide?
FANNY CROSBY

Precious Jesus:

How wonderful it is to know that I will never be lost in the woods, searching, struggling to find the way – not as long as I stay close to your side. Though the path is sometimes hidden by underbrush and vines, and the light is often obscured by the towering trees on every side, I know that I'm safer with you than anywhere I could be on my own.

Amen.

The Rings Tell All

This is what the Lord says, . . . "I will heal my
people and will let them enjoy abundant peace
and security."
JEREMIAH 33:2,6

As you take an invigorating walk along the mountain path by your cabin, you may come across the exposed trunk of a fallen tree. Did you know you can learn the age of the tree by the number of rings in a cross section of wood? During spring, trees take on growth between bark and trunk, resulting in a ring of light wood. In the fall when growth slows down, a ring of darker wood develops, if you look closely at the rings, you'll see they're not all the same size. Thin rings denote a period of drought and slow growth, while wide rings indicate a period of favorable climate and rapid growth. Within some rings you might see signs of insect infestation or disease that the tree successfully fended off while continuing to grow. A tree's rings invite you to explore its rich history.

Deep within your heart, you carry emotional scars from past hurts and sorrows. God sees those things, even if everyone else has long forgotten them. And if you look closely, you'll realize those old scars no longer affect or infect your growth now. They have healed. Seasons of abundant joy have followed those periods of heartbreaking loss, and you have grown beyond the hurt, beyond the pain. God has touched you and sealed the wound so you can keep growing and once again enjoy wholeness of life.

Perhaps you seek the solace of the mountains to soothe a wound not quite healed that has consumed months, years, or even decades of your life in drought. A few days of peace and forgetfulness might temporarily take away some of the sting, but only your God has the power to heal your wound and begin the process of rich new growth. Only he can restore your health so you can keep growing and enjoy the peace of mind he wants for you. Why not ask him?

O Lord my God, I called to you for help and you healed me. O Lord, you brought me up from the grave; you spared me from going down into the pit.

PSALM 30:2-3

No one ever looks in vain to the great physician.
F. F. BOSWORTH

Heavenly Father:

Thank you for being there, seeing me through every difficult, painful time in my life. Your healing touch has healed my broken heart over and over again. You've helped me ward off discouragement and hopelessness and infused me with your living, life-giving water. The rings of my heart tell the story of your love and care.

Amen.

Twinkle, Twinkle

[Jesus said.] "In my Father's house are many rooms. If it were not so, I would have told you. I am going there to prepare a place for you. And if I go and prepare a place for you. I will come back and take you to be with me that you also may be where I am."

JOHN 14:2-3

Tonight, look up into the heavens from your deck. There in the mountains, far from the glare of city lights, you have a front-row seat at a spectacular sky show: brilliant stars, vivid planets, haunting moon. The sky's shimmering lamps seem close enough to touch. The distance from Earth to the moon, however, averages around 240,000 miles. The nearest planet Mars, at its closest to Earth, orbits about 55 million miles away. And our closest star—the sun—shines from approximately 93 million miles up in the sky.

For some people, heaven drifts someplace out there in space, beyond the moon and stars. At the funeral of a loved one, heaven might seem to move close enough for a sentimental nod in its direction, but otherwise it veers out of consciousness. Not so with God's people. Heaven is present now by faith. Heaven is present in you by faith.

For the Christian heaven holds the promise of living with God and all his saints for eternity. That brings you peace of mind and serenity of soul now. Jesus Christ won your place in his family, flight now, you're living your relationship with him on earth. When he calls you home, you will live your relationship with him in heaven. Either way, you are his and he is yours.

As you wrap yourself around the stars tonight, let their distance remind you of the place he has prepared for you. glorious beyond your wildest imagination. Let their closeness speak to you of the presence of God in your life . . . of the heaven you live and breathe every day as his beloved child.

Never again will they hunger never again will they thirst. The sun will not heat upon them, nor any scorching heat. For the Lamb at the center of the throne will be their shepherd: he will lead them to springs of living water. And God will wipe away every tear from their eyes.
REVELATION 7:16-17

Heaven will be the perfection we have always longed for. All the things that made earth unlovely and tragic will be absent in heaven.
BILLY GRAHAM

O Father:

I look forward with great joy to the day when I will see you face to face in the place you have prepared for me. I take hold of it even now by faith and thank you for it. Already your goodness seems more than I could ask or think What will it look like then?

Amen.

A Sure Thing

Let us hold unswervingly to the hope we profess,
for he who promised is faithful.
HEBREWS 10:23

"Oh, I hope I can make it to the top," pants a hiker midway up a steep and rock trail. With sore feet and aching muscles, the hiker has good reason to wonder whether or not he'll be among those who reach the summit of the mountain. It's not a sure thing.

You place your hope in God, but not the uncertain hope of the hapless hiker. In his Word, God has shown you his path and the direction he wants you to take. Yes, sometimes the way gets steep and you face barriers, crevasses, and canyons that make you believe the way impassable. Sometimes you tire in mind and body, and you're tempted to say, "I just can't make it any further." God knows all the obstacles along your path and he knows your strength and endurance. Therefore, he helps. He comes to your aid in the form of his Spirit, who increases your faith . . . by the hand of a friend who helps you out . . . in the discovery of a bridge that allows you to move past the hardship and forward on your journey. This is the kind of assistance he promises you, and it's the kind of assistance that makes you say with confidence, "I place my hope in him." Though you can't yet see the summit, you proclaim with certainty. "My hope is sure. In him, I will make it to the top."

God has promised to take you to the summit—eternal life with him in heaven. He has also promised to help you get there. You might not always know how. You might not see a rescue squad rushing to your aid right now. Nonetheless, you know he's going to come through for you. You know he will never leave you stranded on any part of the path. Your hope rests in the fact he has promised you his strength and power. And since he has promised, it's a sure thing.

To you, O Lord, I lift up my soul; in you I trust,
O my God. Do not let me be put to shame,
nor let my enemies triumph over me. No one
whose hope is in you will ever be put to shame.
PSALM 25:1-3

I place no hope in my strength, nor in my works;
bu all my confidence is in God.
FRANCOIS RABELAIS

Dear Lord:

Every time I pray. every time I see you working on my behalf, it fills me with hope that all your other promises are true as well. I look forward without reservation to a future spent with you — both here on earth and in heaven above. What a great and wonderful God you are.

Amen.

Size It Up

Humble yourselves before the Lord,
and he will lift you up.
JAMES 4:40

Ever think of yourself as an important person . . . a pious person . . . a big person compared with everyone else? Then stand at the foot of a mountain. Lean against one of those skyscraper pines. Even if you're a star basketball player, the soaring height of mountains and trees far overshadows your stature. Now edge yourself close to the throne of God. Even if you're on the short list for sainthood, the glory and grandeur of Almighty God overwhelmingly outshines anything you have ever done or ever will do.

Being in the presence of Almighty God is a humbling experience, and your faith in Jesus Christ puts you in the presence of Almighty God. The first time you sense his Spirit overflowing your heart and soul, you know without a doubt he possesses holiness far beyond your ability to be a good person. Compare God's formidable power with your limited strength. Humbling! Measure concepts you can intellectually grasp and competently discuss against the height, depth, and breadth of God's astounding wisdom and understanding. Humbling! For a truthful perspective on your life, assess the totality of your time here on earth and the fact of his eternity. Humbling!

Humbling, yes, but not humiliating. God takes no pleasure in inferiority complexes or self-abasement. God displays his glory in the majesty of the mountains and his power in the events of your life so you will not yield to the folly of putting your hope and trust in anything or anyone — including yourself — other than him. He demonstrates his wisdom and tells you he is eternal so you'll know the kinds of blessings he wants to give you. Humility means you know who you are — one weak person, beloved of Almighty God, whose identity, abilities, and confidence rest in him alone. Let that humbling truth take you to the heights of holiness today.

Not that we are competent in ourselves to claim anything for ourselves, but our competence comes from God.
2 CORINTHIANS 3:5

True humility is not an abject, groveling, self-despising spirit; it is but a right estimate of ourselves as God sees us.
TYRON EDWARDS

Dear Lord:

You are indeed a great and mighty God and I stand in awe of you. Thank you for reaching down from your heavenly throne and redeeming me, taking me from my fallen, hopeless condition and making me your own beloved child. Help me always to remember from what you have saved me.

Amen.

Mighty Tree

If you call out for insight and cry aloud for
understanding and if you look for it as for silver
and search for it as for hidden treasure, then you
will understand the fear of the Lord and find the
knowledge of God.
PROVERBS 2:3-5

Let your eyes move up the mountainside. The trees are magnificent, aren't they? Now consider this: You could no more create a forest from nothing — which God did — than you could create faith from unbelief — which God does. But just as you can water the seed of a tree, protect a sapling from danger, and rest in the shade of its branches, you can nourish the faith God has created in you.

God planted in you the seed of faith. Now, under his inspiration, there's plenty for you to do. First, you'll want to water it. Feed your faith daily by reading and meditating on the living waters of God's Word. Let his Spirit continue his work, of inspiring you through the truths of Holy Scripture, if you don't understand a portion of it, let his Spirit unfold his meaning to you in his own good time as he cultivates deep roots in you. Then, as your faith grows in height and depth, you'll want to protect it from infection and disease. Ungodly language, indecent thoughts, and corrupt behavior undermine the health and soundness of faith and work against the Spirit's effort to build and encourage faith, if you stumble. go to him in repentance, let his forgiveness restore you. and allow his work to resume in you. Finally, after a lifetime under the inspiration of the Holy Spirit, you may well experience a revelation. You'll discover your faith has grown to a mighty tree. Many people—some of them familiar to you, some of them strangers— lean against your unfailing steadiness and strength, take shelter from doubt and fear under the spread of your comfort and guidance, and find rest in the shade of your godliness and peace.

When the Spirit illuminates the heart, then a
part of the man sees which never saw before; a
part of him knows which never knew before, and
that with a kind of knowing which the most
acute thinker cannot imitate. He knows now in a
deep and authoritative way, and what he knows
needs no reasoned proof. His experience of
knowing is above reason, immediate, perfectly
convincing, and inwardly satisfying.
A. W. TOZER

Heavenly Father:

You have inspired faith and hope in my heart. Now I ask that you
would show me how to nurture those qualities in my life, how to
care for them until they become strong and dominant. Most of all, I
want to be pleasing to you in all that I say and do.

Amen.

Roots

In my integrity you uphold me and set me in
your presence forever.
PSALM 41:-12

Mountain trees often have thick trunks and towering height. This tells you the tree has been around awhile. It has withstood periods of drenching rains and long drought. It has survived fire and disease, and it has held its ground in the wake of damaging winds. You're looking at a tree with a sound and sturdy root system.

Your integrity — your ability to hold your ground in all circumstances — depends on the health and strength of your root system. That's why your God wants you deeply rooted in his Word. Throughout your life, you go through seasons of abundance and times of hardship, if you're rooted in the godly principles stated in his Word, you have integrity in both situations. In seasons of abundance, you find it pleasant and easy to abide by his will and his way of doing things. In times of hardship, however, sticking with his principles requires more effort. How easy it is to lie a little, cheat just a bit, place blame on someone else, or cover up the whole thing. But your strong roots help you withstand the temptation. You have God's assurance that he will see you through. You stand firm, even when the force of change takes away cherished hopes and well-laid plans, even when God's way proves the difficult way . . . the unpopular way . . . the costly way.

Without integrity rooted in a heart of godliness, your moral standards, business ethics, and public behavior will be at the mercy of whatever seems right at the moment. As the nineteenth-century minister and social reformer Henry Ward Beecher once remarked, "Expedients are for the hour; principles for the ages."

God made you not for the hour, but for the ages. Root yourself in godly integrity. Ground yourself firmly in his principles, and you will stand for eternity.

He who walks righteously and speaks what is right,
who rejects gain from extortion and keeps his hand
from accepting bribes, who stops his ears against plots
of murder and shuts his eyes against contemplating
evil – this is the man who will dwell on the heights,
whose refuge will be the mountain fortress. His bread
will be supplied, and water will not fail him.
ISAIAH 33:15-16

Integrity is the noblest possession.
LATIN PROVERB

Heavenly Father:

It is my prayer that I would always be pleasing to you, that I could live in such a way that you would be proud to call me your child. In my heart, I know I will need your help even for that. On my own I will surely wander and discredit your holy name – but with your Holy Spirit to guide and correct me, I believe that I can honor you through my life.

Amen.

His Story

For in Christ all the fullness of the Deity lives in
bodily form, and you have been given fullness in
Christ, who is the head over every power and
authority.
COLOSSIANS 2:9-10

Y ou've found a sheltered spot near your mountain cabin where you can build a campfire. Now you're sitting around it under the starry canopy, toasting marshmallows, and telling stories with family and friends. Entertaining and fun stories told and retold in the shadow of a crackling fire bring people together in a heartwarming and foot-warming experience.

Imagine the stories the shepherds must have told around the campfire after the angels announced the birth of Christ and they took their pilgrimage to meet the newborn King. What stories that same Jesus must have told as he and his disciples cooked fish over a campfire along the shores of the Sea of Galilee—stories about beggars and rich men, lost coins and a pearl of great price. Then those same disciples told stories around the campfire as they recalled how their Jesus had been crucified, buried, and entrusted to the grave until he rose from the dead and showed himself to them.

Jesus has meaning and relevance for you well beyond those familiar Bible stories, however. The stories attest to the fact that God the Son knows what it's like to be human, to be tempted, undergo struggles, feel hunger, and need rest. That means you can approach him with any challenge in your life, and he will know exactly what you're going through. Though innocent of any sin, he took on himself the guilt of all sin and served its penalty—death. His resurrection from the tomb proved his power over death and his desire and ability to restore you to new life. As his redeemed child, you have access to Jesus' forgiveness, compassion, and love every day of your life.

As the campfire gives way to the rays of the morning sun, cherish the happy memories and give thanks for the true and eternal story of Jesus and his everlasting love for you.

Christ was sacrificed once to take away the sins
of many people; and he will appear a second time,
not to bear sin, but to bring salvation to those
who are waiting for him.
HEBREWS 9:28

Jesus did not come to make God's love possible,
but to make God's love visible.
AUTHOR UNKNOWN

Heavenly Father:

Thank you for sending Jesus down to earth that I might one day
live with you in heaven. As I recall the story of the Lord's birth,
death, and resurrection, I am filled with amazement that your Son
would so willingly agree to give up his glory for the cross of
Calvary. I will praise you in this life and the life to come.

Amen.

Care–less Joy

[God] will yet fill your mouth with laughter and
your lips with shouts of joy.
JOB 8:24

As you follow mountain trails, you're on the lookout for interesting and unusual things. You glimpse a deer as she scampers into a cover of ferns and vines. You stop to hear the fluted song of a bird hidden in among the silver leaves of a towering poplar. You stoop to examine a blossom peeking out from the cradle of a sheltered nook. You pick up a leaf to study its shape and color and feel its texture between your fingers. You savor your walk in the mountains because you know you'll make discoveries, and in the thrill and freshness of each discovery, you find joy.

What's true in the mountains remains true in the plains. Trouble is, it's easy to stop being on the lookout for joy when you're dashing down the street you live on or rushing to the grocery store you visit several times a week. You don't expect to see anything interesting or discover anything not there the day before and the day before that. It would be easy to start thinking that joy only exists on the mountaintops. But that simply isn't true.

Joy requires attentive seeing, mindful listening, and willingness to pause, reach out, and discover delight in familiar things. The afternoon sun painting the valley below you also lights your window back home. The majestic mountain pines have fantastic relatives where you live . . .

and while house sparrows may sound less melodic than their forest cousins, they were designed by the same creative hand. All are messages of everyday joy to you from God — from the exotic orchid growing in the cleft of a rock to the common pansy sitting in a window box.

Happiness is fleeting. Happiness cares where you are, how you feel, and what's going on around you. Joy, however, is care-less. God created the world, and he made joy available to everyone. True joy requires only a heart open to the simple blessings of every day.

Shout for joy to the Lord, all the earth.
Worship the Lord with gladness;
come before him with joyful songs.
PSALM 100:1-2

Joy is the most infallible sign of the presence of God.
LEON BLOY

Lord God:

My heart sings as I look around me at your marvelous creation. You truly are great and mighty. Why you would choose to have a relationship with me, I do not know — but you do and that fills my heart to overflowing with joy, gratitude, and peace. Thank you, Lord.

Amen.

Nature's Way

The fruit of the Spirit is love, joy, peace, patience,
kindness, goodness, faithfulness, gentleness, and
self control. Against such things there is no law.
GALATIANS 5:22-23

You can judge the health of a tree by looking at its branches. In summer, leafless branches point to an infestation of pests or the presence of disease. In winter, brown pine needles indicate blight or the adverse effects of harsh climate conditions. Withered leaves, blackened fruit, and other signs serve as nature's way of telling you something is wrong with the tree.

Jesus compared his relationship to believers with that of a vine to its branches. As long as believers, the branches, hold firmly to him, the vine, they will bear good fruit. Firm, sweet fruit hanging from sturdy branches attests to the soundness of the vine. Withered, sour fruit shows you the branch is not attached to a healthy plant.

Do you ever find yourself wondering whether or not you're attached to Jesus? After all, you can't see faith, even your own. Once down from the mountain top excitement of becoming a Christian, believers often question the quality and depth of their faith. Is it healthy faith? Is it thriving . . . or wilting under pressure?

Take time to examine the fruit of faith in your life. Are the spiritual fruit of love, joy, peace, patience, kindness, goodness, gentleness, faithfulness, and self-control (see Gal.

5:22) maturing in your heart and life? Are they substantial enough to be seen by others? You be the judge—and if you find yourself wanting, ask God to securely attach you to the vine, where you live and breathe in constant communion with Jesus. You will have the joy of knowing that you are pleasing to him.

I am the vine; you are the branches. If a man remains in me and I in him, he will bear much fruit; apart from me you can do nothing.
JOHN 15:5

God is more concerned about our character than our comfort. His goal is not to pamper us physically, but to perfect us spiritually.
PAUL W. POWELL

Heavenly Father:

I desire that the fruit of the Spirit be apparent in my life so that everyone around will know that you and I are in vital union. Show me, Lord, if there is anything in my life that helps me from being a strong, healthy branch in your vine.

Amen.

Attention, Please

Listen, my son, accept what I say
and the years of your life will be many.
PROVERBS 4:10

The forest that covers the nearby mountainside teems with critters of the furred and feathered kind. You hear them — the chattering of a chipmunk, the hoot of an owl, the howl of a wolf in the distance. But hush, what's that twittering sound? Who's making such a plaintive call? To hear the subtle voices of the forest, you need to practice attentive listening.

Attentive listening is vital to robust relationships with others and to a vibrant relationship with God. The same three reasons apply to both. First, attentive listening fully focuses on what the other person is saying. It's not distracted by what else is going on or thinking about something else. It hears more than the main topic stated. It hears the meaning of the words both spoken and unspoken. When God speaks to you in his Word or through a consecrated human voice, focus your attention on him alone. Hear his words as well as his whispers. Second, attentive listening leaves no room for formulating a reply while the other person speaks. It never interrupts or rushes in with its censure, advice, or opinion. Though your exposure to God speaking in his Word confronts you with uncomfortable truths and challenging commandments, hush! Hear him out. When he has finished speaking, let the Spirit guide your thoughtful and well-considered response. Third, attentive listening applies what's being said. It builds a bridge between speaker and listener by finding connections between the two and being teachable, willing to hear a new perspective and explore new areas. What holds true for communication between you and other people holds doubly true for communication between you and God. Apply what he says to your life. Find ways to make his words real by doing what he says: that's one of the reasons he's talking to you!

Your attentive listening picks up more than hoots and howls of words; it also picks up the subtle chirps and quiet breathings of the Spirit at work in you.

Pay attention and listen to the sayings of the wise;
apply your heart to what I teach, for it is pleasing
when you keep them in your heart and have all of them
ready on your lips.
PROVERBS 22:17-18

Lord, teach me to silence my own heart that I may
listen to the genre movement of the Holy Spirit within
me and sense the depths which are of God.
ELIJAH DE VIDAS

Dear Lord:

Help me tune my heart to hear your voice — your mighty words of power and authority, as well as those words you speak with a still, small voice. I don't want to miss a single word. Thank you, Lord, for speaking to me and being patient when I in distracted and fail to hear you.

Amen.

Get Real

*As God's chosen ones, holy and beloved, clothe
yourselves with compassion, kindness, humility,
meekness, and patience . . . Above all, clothe
yourselves with love, which binds everything together
in perfect harmony.*
COLOSSIANS 3:12, 14 NRSV

If this is the first time you've visited the mountains, it probably took you just a few minutes to realize that reality is pretty different than the ideal extolled in glossy photos and shiny brochures. The ideal may have caught your attention, helped you make the decision to come, but the real thing keeps you there, feeding your soul with the sights and sounds of this truly amazing place.

The same applies to love. Everyone knows what ideal love looks like: images described in fairy tales and romance novels. The experience of life quickly dispels such a sentimental haze. Parents fail. A spouse turns cold. Children make poor choices. Friends change. Some people can't deal with love's realities. When they learn that real love brings all the ups and downs, the bliss and the trials, the excitement and sameness of any other earthly experience, they turn around and head in the other direction. They don't realize that love, though never ideal, is always worth it.

When God commanded his people to love one another, he knew the difference between real and ideal. He knew how hard it can be to love if trust has been betrayed, if kindness has been repaid with insult, if goodwill resulted in offense. He knew that if his people were to extend real love to one another, they would have to forgive one another, bear with one another, be patient With one another. Without a willingness to give and receive these things, love remains a sentimental ideal. With them, love becomes a real-life experience.

What if you had turned around and gone home the minute you realized the brochure's ideal picture was a shallow cover? Happily, you didn't act on hasty judgments. So why let love remain in your imagination? To make it real, all it takes is willingness to give love a chance.

Love is patient, love is kind. It does not envy, it does not boast, it is not proud. It is not rude, it is not self seeking, it is not easily angered, it keeps no record of wrongs. Love does not delight in evil but rejoices with the truth.

1 CORINTHIANS 13:4-6

It is only inasmuch as you see someone else as he or she really is here and now, and not as they are in our memory or desire or in your imagination or projection, that you can truly love them.

ANTHONY DE MELLO

Dear Father:

I want to give and receive real love — not the kind that comes from fairy tales and feel-good stories, but the kind of love that flows from you, the kind that survives adversity and overlooks offenses. I thank you, Lord, for your great example of real, lasting love.

Amen.

A Comforting Thought

God, who is rich in mercy, out of the great love with
which he loved us even when we were dead through
our trespasses, made us alive together with Christ.
EPHESIANS 2: 4-5 NRSV

Nature shows no mercy. A rockslide cascading down a mountain crushes everything in its path. Forest fires torch ancient trees and tender saplings alike. The force of a flooded stream tears up the nests of roosting birds and washes away branches, logs, stepping stones, and bridges.

God's anger swoops down on sin with a power far exceeding the destructive forces of nature, His absolute perfection tolerates neither sin nor anything touched by sin. He makes no differentiation between big sins and little sins, horrendous offenses and slight indiscretions, public scandals and private weaknesses. It's all sin and if sin were to touch perfection, perfection would no longer exist. There's no such thing as purity with a little bit of dirt thrown in! No sin can withstand the power of God's wrath, and no sin is an exception. Not a comforting thought.

Unlike the forces of blind nature, God sees and has mercy. Born on this earth, you cannot avoid being infected and affected by your own sins and the sins of others. You can't protect yourself from the calamities of a sinful world. You won't find a loophole allowing you to slip away from God's judgment on sin. Your only help rests in mercy—his mercy. Jesus came to pull you out of the way of God's wrath by taking sin's punishment on himself. The perfect Son of God endured God's wrath on the cross and earned your perfection when he rose from the grave. Even though you commit sins and you feel the effects of sin, your forgiveness in Jesus assures you of your safe and secure place far beyond the boundaries of God's wrath. Because of Jesus, God looks at you and he's not angry. He doesn't see sin. Instead, he sees his beloved child robed in the perfection of Jesus Christ. Lord, have mercy! And he does. Now there's a comforting thought.

> *For the Lord your God is a merciful God: he will*
> *not abandon or destroy you or forget the*
> *covenant with your forefathers, which he*
> *confirmed to them by oath.*
> *DEUTERONOMY 4:31*

> *God giveth his wrath by weight, but his mercy*
> *without measure.*
> *SIR THOMAS FULLER*

Heavenly Father:

I hate to think where I would be without your mercy. Clearly, I would not have your presence in my life, and I feel that would be a loss I could never bear. Thank you for your mercy demonstrated by Jesus' sacrifice for me on the cross. I owe everything to him and to you for loving me enough to pay the price for my purity.

Amen.

Growth at the Top

The goal of this command is love, which comes from a pure heart and a good conscience and a sincere faith.
1 TIMOTHY 1:5

This morning you've wandered from the cabin down the trail to where a stand of thick, dense trees are standing. You aren't sure what type they are, but they stand out from the tall, slender mountain pines. You step carefully under the canopy of heavy branches and notice immediately that the sun barely enters here. Layers of fallen twigs, leaves, branches, and pine needles crackle under your feet. Apparently, moisture is as obstructed as light in this leafy wonderland. That would explain why there seems to be little new growth on the forest floor.

Did you know that your heart can mimic the conditions in that dark, dry forest? As you gain spiritual maturity and become experienced in the ways of God, it's easy to develop certain ideas and expectations. For example, what kind of worship service best pleases him? What conduct marks real Christians? Which sort of people truly belong to him? Which political opinions reflect God's point of view? Whose prayers does he really hear? All these things fall around the base of your faith, and, with time, overshadow the refreshing and renewing light of God's wisdom and understanding. Layers of personal judgment and individual preference snuff out insights offered by others as well as any deeper understanding of your own through continued study of

God's Word. Conditions within your heart simply aren't open to new growth.

If you think this describes you, take a look at a spreading oak, a dense fir, a towering' sequoia. Now look up to the top of the tree. Green leaves. New branches. Life—where it's open to rainfall and sunshine. The same holds true for you. With your roots firmly in Christ and secure in his Word, look up. Reach out to his life-giving waters and open yourself to the ever-renewing light of his wisdom and love.

This is my prayer: that your love may abound more and more in knowledge and depth of insight, so that you may be able to discern what is best and may be pure and blameless until the day of Christ.
PHILIPPIANS 1:9-10

Sincerity is an openness of heart.
FRANCOIS ROCHEFOUCAULD

Dear Father:

I don't want to be the kind of Christian who escapes under the canopy of religion and doesn't seek the sunshine of personal relationship with you or feel the life-giving moisture that comes from having an open mind to insights from your Word. Help me to expose my faith to your light so that I may continue growing as a believer.

Amen.

Are We There Yet?

If we hope for what we do not yet have,
we wait for it patiently.
ROMANS 8:25

If you drove to the mountains and the kids rode in the back seat, you heard it, if your parents used to drive you and your siblings just about anywhere, you said it. "Are we there yet?" Once they leave the driveway, kids can't wait to get where they're going— where the fun begins. As an adult, you know the process of getting there holds its own experiences and discoveries. There's the adventure of the open road and the passing sights of fields and farms, towns and waterways as you pass through desert and prairie to your destination. You urge your young ones to be patient while you point out to them all there is to see and learn along the way.

When you're going through a time of hardship, patience doesn't come easily. You want to get to the end of it. You beg God to lift your burden, but nothing changes. "God, are we there yet?" Does he hear you? Is he aware of your situation? Are you on an endless trip to nowhere? These thoughts crowd into your mind, turning your eyes away from the road, away from the scenery, away from God. But out of your despondency, God brings you his sure and certain promises: "I hear you. I know where you are. And yes, you have a destination. Be patient while I take you there!" Along the way, God encourages you to learn and discover what he has in mind for you. He points out new opportunities for you to grow in perseverance, compassion, and understanding. He show's you how he works in you during challenging times. His Spirit prompts remembrance of his promises and reliance on his care.

Are you there yet? No, not if you're still lacing the challenge. God has some more things to show you along the way, Be patient. He holds the itinerary and has the timetable . . . and he's the Driver.

Be patient ... until the Lord's coming. See how the farmer waits for the land to yield its valuable crop and how patient he is for the autumn and spring rains. You too, be patient and stand firm, because the Lord's coming is near.
JAMES 5:7-8

Teach us, O Lord, the discipline of patience, for to wait is often harder than to work.
PETER MARSHALL

Heavenly Father:

I know I have trouble waiting. I always want to be where we're going right away. Thank you for speaking to my heart that the journey is as important as the destination. Point out to me the exciting possibilities along the way and give me a patient heart!

Amen.

Ever-Present Peace

A heart at peace gives life to the body.
PROVERBS 14:30

Perhaps you're attracted to the mountains because you have found there a sense of serenity and a chance to reconnect with God. You wouldn't be the first. Jesus, during his ministry on earth, frequently went up to a mountain for a period of seclusion, prayer, and peace. And you certainly aren't the last. The timeless beauty of the forest, meandering mountain paths, shady coves, and stunning lookouts provides the perfect setting for meditation and relaxation. For physical, mental, and spiritual peace.

Despite the unparalleled peace Jesus no doubt found on the mountain, he didn't stay there. After a time of refreshment, he came down from the mountain and went back to work. He taught crowds of eager listeners and healed their sick. He deftly handled the slippery questions put to him by people trying to trip him up, and he boldly faced the soldiers who came to the garden of Gethsemane to arrest him. He knew the soldiers would shortly lead him up another mountain, and this would not prove a peaceful visit. On the hill called Calvary, they nailed him to a cross and there he died—and rose again to ensure our peace for an eternal lifetime.

While you're up in the mountains, you have his peace in your tranquil surroundings and in the quietness of your soul.

Down on the plain, you have his peace as you go about your life with Christ-centered confidence, respond to challenges with godly decisions and choices, and overcome temptation with his ever-present help. When you're in him, his peace is yours . . . anywhere.

The fruit of righteousness will be peace; the effect of righteousness will be quietness and confidence forever.
ISAIAH 32:17

The fruit of placing all things in his hands is the presence of his abiding peace in our hearts.
HANNAH WHITALL SMITH

Heavenly Father:

Your peace is one of my most treasured possessions. When the world around me is spinning, I can close my eyes and think about you, and my peace is as certain as if I were looking down on my situation from a quiet mountainside. Thank you for giving me your peace that is constant no matter what is happening in my life.

Amen.

Steep Slopes and Aching Feet

Let us not become weary in doing good, for at the proper time we will reap a harvest if we do not give up.

GALATIANS 6:9

On a long hike to the lop of the mountain, muscles begin to ache. Perhaps you decide to rest a little bit before pushing on again. Or you grab a good sturdy stick to lean on as you walk. Or you let up your pace a bit. If you want to reach the summit, however, you need to keep going. You can reach it no other way but through perseverance.

If you're like most people, you learned perseverance after you realized that quitting doesn't get you where you want to go. You realized you'll never get to the top of the mountain if you get discouraged on the first hill, or if you lack the willingness to tread a rough trail, if you're committed to reaching a goal, you persevere in your efforts.

Your commitment to Christ requires spiritual perseverance. Many times along the path of discipleship, you will get tired— expect it. All of his people tire at one time or another, no matter where they are on their journey. For this reason, your Lord walks with you. He refreshes you with his loving promises to you so you remain steady on your feet. You might find yourself facing a steep slope or a patch of rough road. He gives you his Spirit to support you so you can manage difficulties and overcome barriers ahead of you. You might need to slow down a little—things aren't working out as you thought they would. The direction you were headed doesn't seem to be the one he had in mind for you. That's okay. He'll take you up in his arms and put you back on his path. Then he wants you to move forward—to persevere.

If you're tired, go to your Lord for help and refreshment. He restores sore muscles and massages hurt feet. He renews commitment and makes perseverance possible. In him and with him, you'll reach the summit.

You need to persevere so that when you have
done the will of God, you will receive what he
has promised.
HEBREWS 10:36

Great works are performed, not by strength,
but by perseverance.
SAMUEL JOHNSON

Heavenly Father:

Lately I've felt my resolve ebbing away as I work toward the
dreams you've placed in my life. I need your help as I commit anew
to stay the course, overcome discouragement, and trust that you
will strengthen me and walk with me on the remainder of my
journey. Thank you, Lord.

Amen.

Better Plans

The plans of the Lord stand firm forever, the
purposes of his heart through all generations.
PSALM 33: 11

"If you want to make God laugh, just tell him your plans." The old saying puts plans — even the most well-thought-out plans — into proper perspective.

No matter how well you planned your mountain vacation, in all likelihood you've had to make some adjustments. The plane didn't depart on time, and you didn't make your connecting flight. Road construction necessitated a detour thirty' miles out of your way. It rained the day you had planned to go fishing. It's unlikely you spent too much time pouting about your old plans. You handled the situation by making new ones.

New plans in response to incidental delays, unexpected detours, and bad weather are fairly easy to make. But when big plans go awry in a major way. change comes less easily and with much more emotional trauma. An unforeseen job change or an unexpected relocation forces you to rewrite long-term goals and reevaluate things you thought were set for the future. Debilitating illness in the family, the loss of a spouse, a parent's needs, or a child's emotional problems push your plans into the background. Then does God laugh? No, of course not. His love and care for you wouldn't allow him to do so. He does, however, have some words of comfort and encouragement for you when your plans fall through. He tells you in no uncertain terms: "My plans for you are great plans."

Your plans may have been quite good and notably responsible ones. And certainly you should make plans for your future based on the knowledge and experience you possess today. But when God sends a delay, routes you to another road, or changes the climate completely, give thanks for what he puts in front of you. Maybe even laugh. When God hands you his plans, you're getting the great ones.

"I know the plans I have for you," announces the Lord. "I want you to enjoy success. I do not plan to harm you. I will give you hope for the years to come."
JEREMIAH 29:11 NIRV

I find that doing the will of God leaves me no time for disputing about his plans.
GEORGE MACDONALD

Lord God:

You know I'm one of those people who has a plan for every thing. I don't like it much when things go off track. Help me to be more flexible — flexible enough to accept the delays and detours front my plans that keep me on track with your plans. Thank you for loving me enough to reroute me for my own good.

Amen.

Bad Bear

Before they call I will answer; while they are still
speaking I will hear.
ISAIAH 65:24

The story goes that a camper was cornered by a bear. His wife grabbed a basket of food to lure the bear away, but the camper cried. "No need to do that. I'm praying. God will send a miracle." A park ranger came upon the scene and immediately produced a tranquilizer dart to disable the bear, but the camper cried out again, saying. "Don't shoot! I'm praying. God will send a miracle." Soon a lifeline helicopter buzzed overhead and a medic lowered a rope to the man, but he refused the offer, again citing the imminent miracle. The bear won the contest and the man found himself at the pearly gates. "Why didn't God send a miracle to rescue me from the bear?" he asked Saint Peter. "He sent you three," replied Saint Peter. "He sent a basket of food, a tranquilizer dart, and a rope."

When you pray, God answers. But do you recognize his answers? They're not always in the way, shape, or form you might think. His unequivocal yes might be present in your life right now, but you're looking to the wrong person for it. His compassionate *no* might have come with something else much better for you, but you're stubbornly holding out for your original idea. His *not yet* could point to the best thing that could happen to you when you're ready for it, but you're unhappy over not getting your way right now.

You are free—even invited—to approach your heavenly Father with all your needs and desires, your wishes and dreams. But when you get up off your knees, open your eyes as you look for his answers. Reach out and accept what he sends you with gladness and gratitude. And if you're cornered by a bear today, remember the rules. Don't run; slowly back away, and grab the first miracle God throws out to you!

[Jesus said.] "Ask and it will be given to you:
seek and you will find; knock and the door will be
opened to you. For everyone who asks receives,
he who seeks finds; and to him who knocks, the
door will he opened."
MATTHEW 7:7-8

All who call on God in true faith, earnestly from
the heart, will certainly be heard and will receive
what they have asked and desired.
MARTIN LUTHER

Dear Lord:

I know I've been guilty of overlooking your answers to my prayers
at times. Like a stubborn child. I say I don't like carrots, I want
candy. Thanks for opening my eyes to what I've been doing, for I
know that now I will see more clearly. Your answers are best for
me and come in your perfect timing. Thank you, Lord

Amen.

First Things First

He who pursues righteousness and
love finds life, prosperity and honor.
PROVERBS 21:21

As you planned your vacation, you no doubt made one activity your priority. Maybe it was to embark on an all-day wilderness walk. Maybe it was to spend every morning out on the lake with your fishing rod. Or sit on the deck of your cabin with sketch pad and charcoal pencil. You may have wanted to simply relax and take in the peacefulness around you. Right now. any onlooker can tell where your priority lies, because that's what you're spending most of your time doing.

God invites you to make him the priority of your life. A sure way to know if you are, in fact, making him your priority is to act as your own onlooker, watch yourself for a week—if you enter each day with a prayer of praise and thanksgiving to God and commit yourself each night to his protection and care, you're putting him first in your thoughts and mind, if your conduct throughout the day reflects his Spirit's gifts of gentleness, kindness, patience, and self-control, you're putting him first in the things you do and say. If you willingly assist others in their needs and joyfully support them in their successes, you're putting him first in your relationships. if you faithfully worship him and contribute to the work of his kingdom, you're putting him first in your time and resources, if you pray—always pray— you're putting him first in your heart. If you see yourself doing these things out of love for him. rather than obligation, he is the priority of your life,

Why do you think God asks you to make him your life's priority? In his Word, he tells you why: it's so he can give you everything you need in life and much, much more, and so you will know from whom these things have come. In Jesus, God made you number one with him. In your life, make sure you can see he's Number One with you.

> *[Jesus said,] "Seek first his kingdom and his righteousness, and all these things will be given to you as well."*
> *MATTHEW 6:33*

> *When you put God first, you are establishing order for everything else in your life.*
> *ANDREA GARNEY*

Dear Father:

I know I have a long way to go before all the areas of my life are in proper order. I will need your help. I want you to know, though, that it's my desire to place you in that number one spot. I know that with you there, my other priorities will fall into place and I'll have much success in all I do. Thank you. Lord, for training my heart to put you first.

Amen.

Daily Bread

*If anyone is in Christ, he is a new creation, the
old has gone, the new has come!*
2 CORINTHIANS 5:17

I f you're an early riser, you savor the sight of dawn's
first rays breaking through the muted shadows of
the forest. You appreciate the serenade of the
brightening sky and the melody of the first chirps of birds
roused from their nests by the light. As the sun rises, a new
beginning unfolds. "God had infinite time to give us." said
Ralph Waldo Emerson. "He cut it up into a neat succession
of new mornings, and, with each, therefore, a new idea, new
inventions, and new applications."

With each new day comes renewal of mind and body, of
opportunity and purpose. With each new day comes renewal
of soul too. Regardless of what happened yesterday, God
starts over with you with each new dawn. When the light of
his forgiveness lifts the darkness of sin. the darkness is no
more. God is not going to plunge you into midnight at noon,
nor is he going to mingle his day with sin's night. Because of
Jesus' sacrifice on the cross to win your forgiveness, you live
in the day. He has renewed you. In addition, God renews
you by using each day to bring you forward on your
spiritual walk with him. Look around you. In today's fresh
light, do you see a new way to show love and compassion to
others? Listen. Do you hear anything around you that sparks
an idea of how you can use your gifts more fully in his

service? Renewal brings with it new eyes . . . new ears . . . new ways to live out your spiritual calling in this world.

You came to the mountains to get away from everyday routine . . . for renewal. When you go back home, you'll feel refreshed and ready to go again, perhaps even with an added spring in your step. For spiritual renewal, though, don't wait until you're able to climb to a mountaintop. In the light of Jesus' love, you have renewal in him every day of your life.

> *I will give you a new heart and put a new spirit*
> *in you; I will remove from you your heart of*
> *stone and give you a heart of flesh. And I will*
> *put my Spirit in you and move you to follow my*
> *decrees and be careful to keep my laws.*
> *EZEKIEL 36:26-27*

> *We can provide for ourselves a new haircut, new*
> *clothing, but only God can give us a new day*
> *and a restored soul.*
> *ANDREA GARNEY*

Dear Lord:

Thank you for your mercy and grace. Thank you for forgiveness and new beginnings. Thank you for your matchless goodness. Each day I will raise my head and lift my eyes and praise you for the bright morning of a new day.

Amen.

Rest for the Weary

[Jesus said,] "Come to me, all you who are weary
and burdened, and I will give you rest."
MATTHEW 11:28

"I need to get some rest!" Perhaps you came to the mountains with the specific intention of getting some needed rest. If you're like most adults, the number of your commitments, responsibilities, and other activities add up to weeks, if not months, of long days and short nights. To really find rest, you need to get away for a while and leave your to-do list behind.

Jesus offers you rest of a different kind. His rest doesn't take you away from it all—or take it all away from you. You've probably noticed he rarely answers your cries for a break from your trials with a one-way ticket out of them. You might even have felt disappointed and somewhat let down if, after deep and fervent prayer on your part, Jesus failed to do his part and remove your troubles from you. Things remained as before, with no immediate vacation from the source of your sorrow or the cause of your suffering. Why? Because Jesus' idea of rest goes far deeper than anything a quick change of scenery or sudden shift in circumstances could possibly provide. Jesus offers to give you spiritual rest, the kind of rest that keeps you in his peace through the night's storms and the day's stresses wherever you are and whenever they happen. In his rest, you'll handle your challenges and you'll address your struggles, but not by getting as far away from them as you can. There's no need. When you rest in Jesus, he takes you through them in peace.

Shady trees, secluded pathways, quiet ponds, and meandering streams make the perfect setting for a much-needed reprieve from the demands of a full calendar. But for a place of rest once you resume your busy schedule, turn to Jesus. He'll take you where you need to go — directly to him and the skelter and strength of his arms.

Let the beloved of the Lord rest secure in him, for
he shields him all day long, and the one the Lord
loves rests between his shoulders.
DEUTERONOMY 33:12.

No soul can have rest until it finds created
things are empty. When the soul gives up all for
love, so that it can have him that is all. Then it
finds true rest.
JULIAN OF NORWICH

Precious Father:

Thank you for real, lasting, complete rest — rest for every part of me. Even when I can't break away, which is most of the time, you bring what I need to my heart. You offer to help me carry my burdens and refresh my troubled soul. You are my oasis in the desert, my refuge from the storm. Thank you, Lord.

Amen.

Perfect Sight

*It was a perfect sacrifice by a perfect person to perfect
some very imperfect people. By that single offering.
[Christ] did everything that needed to be done for
everyone who takes part in the purifying process.*
HEBREWS 10:13-14 MSG

Someone once said that people who seek perfection in their lives are setting themselves up for failure. A relentless pursuit of perfection in even small and insignificant things invites disappointment. What if you refused to admire the beauty of a stately pine until you happened on a perfect specimen? What if you wouldn't take your boat out and fish until conditions on the lake proved flawless? What if you refused to enjoy the breathtaking view of the mountains as long as they were shrouded in mist or low-hanging clouds? Chances are, you would find little to love about your vacation.

People who set their sights on being perfect find little to love about themselves. With great effort, they faithfully adhere to a strict code of ethics and uphold a high standard of personal morality. But what about their haunting misgivings that they haven't done quite enough—that their behavior has not shown itself faultless in every circumstance? What about the needling uneasiness of heart and soul when doubt and suspicion stir the pristine waters of their hard-earned peace? What about the moment they honestly face the fact that human beings just aren't capable of perfection?

Only God can make perfection happen. His perfect Son, Jesus, took on the imperfections of all people so all who believe in Jesus become perfect in God's sight. Jesus' sacrifice for you saves you from worrying about becoming perfect, because in God's eyes you are perfect already. His forgiveness of your sins relieves you from trying to hide or deny your imperfections, because God isn't looking at them. When God sees you, he sees perfection. He sees everything to love about you.

He saved us not because of righteous things we had done, but because of his mercy. He saved us through the washing of rebirth and renewal by the Holy Spirit, whom he poured out on us generously through Jesus Christ our Savior, so that, having been justified by his grace, we might become heirs having the hope of eternal life.

TITUS 3:5-7

If there be ground for you to trust in your own righteousness, then all that Christ did to purchase salvation, and all that God did to prepare the way for it, is in vain.

JONATHAN EDWARDS

Lord God:

Teach my restless, care-burdened heart to rest in your love and your righteousness. Help me to accept that I can't live a perfect life, no matter how hard I try, but you are there to wash me clean when I fail so I will always be welcome in your presence.

Amen.

Outstanding in Your Field

Remember this: whoever sows sparingly will also reap
sparingly, and whoever sows generously will also reap
generously.
2 CORINTHIANS 9:6

Y ou stand on the porch of your cabin marveling at the beauty before you. To the left, foothills rise, sweeping up and away, a mountain peak in the distant background. The hillside is draped in a cloak of incredible wildflowers, an abundance of blossoms from the scattered seeds of a few. A flower boasts no brighter color if it keeps its seeds to itself. The only way it becomes a gem in a field of beauty is by giving itself, scattering its seeds. Similarly, seeds of kindness, of gentleness, of love not scattered but hoarded never enrich the possessor and. in the end, leave the world all the drabber.

Your Christian giving involves far more than tithing at church and making donations to charities, as excellent and necessary as those things are in the kingdom of God. Your Christian giving, with its source in Jesus' gift of his life for you, begins when you give of yourself . . . your kindness to family members, to friends, to colleagues and coworkers, to the person standing in front of you at the convenience store. Your willingness to take time for others, to acknowledge them, to care about them, to listen to them, and to assist them even when it's inconvenient for you. Perhaps you had planned to join your friends for the evening, but you know your loved one needs your company right now. Perhaps you've already had to make a choice: the vigorous hike you had set your sights on or the easy walking trail your kids can handle? This kind of giving reaches beyond the wallet, beyond self-interest, beyond requirements. This kind of giving gets to the heart of the matter—it's your response to everything God has given to you.

When you selflessly scatter the seeds of God's love by giving of yourself, you're sowing bright, beautiful blossoms all around you. And when you're standing in the middle of a field of brilliant flowers, you can't help but feel—and look—fantastic.

[Jesus said,] ' Give, and it will be given to you. A good measure, pressed down, shaken together and running over, will be poured into your lap. For with the measure you use. it will be measured to you."

LUKE 6:38

The seed that is sown is scattered with an open hand. The sower in order to have a harvest has to turn loose the seed. He can't grip it in his fist; he can't hesitate to let it go; he can't just sprinkle a little here and there - he's got to generously sow it.

CHARLES SPURGEON

Heavenly Father:

I want to be a giver – a giver of love, kindness, and compassion. I want to give to others as you have so generously given to me. Thank you for filling my heart and life to overflowing and for giving me the privilege of following in your footsteps.

Amen.

Strong Legs on Steep Hills

*It is God who arms me with strength and makes
my way perfect. He makes my feet like the feet of
a deer; he enables me to stand on the heights.*
PSALM 18:32-33

A long hike up a steep hill leaves your knees a little wobbly. Unless you're a trained climber, you'll need to sit down along the way to catch your breath and rest your muscles. If the pain becomes unbearable, you might decide you can climb no farther. Someone striding up to you saying, "Come on, buddy . . . you can do it!" won't help. You need more than a pep talk and positive attitude. You need real strength to continue on.

Many times and in many ways throughout Scripture, God tells his disheartened people, "Be strong! Have courage!" Because these words spring from the mouth of God, you know you're getting more than a fellow hiker's words of encouragement. You're hearing more than a master climber's advice on how to reach the top of the mountain. God's words are endued with power to provide real help, real strength.

When God tells you he will strengthen you—that's exactly what he will do. When you feel yourself weaken in the face of life's trials, he invites you to sit down in his presence and meditate on his promises. When you worry that you can't go on, he asks you to pause and recall how exhausted Jesus was as he carried his cross on the day of his crucifixion. Do you remember the humble man who God used to carry the cross for him? God will provide real help for you as well.

Though the mountain's steep slopes may force you to turn back, or its ravines and canyons prove impossible for you to cross, none of life's challenges lie beyond the strength of the Lord to get you where you're going. In him, you have remarkably strong legs.

Strengthen the feeble hands, steady the knees
that give way; say to those with fearful hearts,
"Be strong, do not fear; your God will come, he
will come with vengeance; with divine
retribution he will come to save you."
ISAIAH 35:3-4

When a man has no strength, if he leans on God,
he becomes powerful.
DWIGHT L. MOODY

Heavenly Father:

I am so tired, so powerless, so out of resources. I need your strength to infuse me more than ever before. I need your powerful arms to lift me up and carry me until I can walk on my own again. Thank you, Lord, that I don't have to face my life alone. You are always with me, always providing exactly what I need.

Amen.

Headed Up

---

*"Not by might nor by power, but by my Spirit," says
the LORD Almighty.*
ZECHARIAH 4:6

On your morning walk, you see fallen oak lying on the forest floor and a bit farther away a fir, twisted and scarred, obviously a victim of disease. The fallen oak will never rise again and the fir will never again grow straight and tall. Nothing in nature prepares you for what the human spirit can do: rise from the depths of addiction . . . from the despair of loss . . . from the brink of self-destruction.

God illustrates resurrection in his Son Jesus Christ, and success in Jesus' victory over sin. Jesus gave up the glories of heaven to bear the poverty of earth. He suffered the disgrace of crucifixion an agonizing, public, and humiliating death reserved for the lowest of the low. But even from the depths of such degradation, God restored life. Jesus rose again. His resurrection means he triumphed over everything the grave has to offer. It means your sins are forgiven, no matter how low these sins may have brought you. It means you can believe in resurrection, because he has risen. For you. he has triumphed over every fall. In him, you can rise again.

When God created the world, he made you different from mountains, canyons, and lakes. He made you different from other living things, like trees, flowers, birds, and animals. When God made you, he gave you an eternal soul. Once that soul is invigorated and redeemed by his Spirit, you are able to rise again from failure, disappointment, hurt, and sorrow. Success lies within you, because he does.

"Your greatest triumphs are not in winning," a wise person once said, "but in rising again after every fall." Jesus rose from the grave and triumphed over all evil, including death, if you're walking in a spiritual canyon right now. reach out to him, because he's willing, ready, and able to raise you up again and prepare you for the kind of success you'll have for eternity·

Though you have made me see troubles, many and
bitter, you will restore my life again; from the depths
of the earth you will again bring me up. You will
increase my honor and comfort me once again.
PSALM 71:20-21

The purpose of revelation is restoration, the renewal in
us of that likeness to God which man lost by sin.
STEPHEN NEILL

Heavenly Father:

You know what I've suffered — every single disappointment and loss. I wonder if there is any hope for me now. Am I too far gone, too twisted and bent and deformed to ever be of value again? I don't know, but I place my hope and trust in you. I ask you to awaken me by your Spirit. Create for me a new beginning. Thank you for lifting me up.

Amen.

Water Works

Submit yourselves then, to God.
Resist the devil, and he will flee from you.
JAMES 4:7

Perhaps you've stood on the bank of a gently flowing stream, the water's murmur as it follows its course down the mountain offers a sense of peace and purpose . . . and aptly illustrates the concept of spiritual surrender.

Before you were born, God planned a course for your life. Before your mother even saw you, you were important to him! To help you follow the path he laid out for you, he put his Word in front of you. There you learned about his commandments and his requirements — things to keep your relationship with him and your relationships with others flowing in the right direction. As he gave the mountain stream its banks, so he put a guard on your left and on your right to hold you and direct you in the way you should go.

Of course, you know what happens when a stream overflows its banks. The stream picks up all sorts of debris that encumbers its travel and muddies its waters. Only when the stream gets back within its banks and surrenders its useless clutter does it flow peacefully and unimpeded to its destination.

God invites you to surrender yourself to him so you can flow freely and peacefully in the way he wants you to go. When you, with the help of his Spirit, forsake your own desires for his commandments and let go of self-seeking, self-interest, and self-indulgence—leaving behind negative thoughts, anger, and dissatisfaction—you will be like a clear, clean mountain stream flowing in its place and toward its purpose. Your God-given course may or may not fill the forests with the roar of a gushing creek or provide the spectacle of a shooting geyser, but your complete surrender to God will certainly bring you God's deep peace and keep you flowing in the path of his divine purpose for your life.

If you devote your heart to him and stretch out your hands to him . . . then you will lift up your face without shame you will stand firm and without fear . . . You will be secure, because there is hope; you will look about you and take your rest in safety.
JOB 11:13,15,18

I have held many things in my hands, and I have lost them all; but whatever I have placed in God's hands, that I still possess.
CORRIE TEN BOOM

Lord God:

Forgive me for the times I have moved outside your will and purpose for my life. I certainly have learned that being outside your protective boundaries is somewhere I don't want to be. Once again, I surrender every aspect of my life to you. I give you full reign to guide my life in the way you think it should go and I do so with complete confidence that you will take me exactly where I need to go.

Amen.

Location, Location, Location

Enter his gates with thanksgiving and his courts
with praise; give thanks to him and praise his
name.

PSALM 100:4

Perhaps you've spotted the peaks of A-frames tucked in the trees and admired (with a tinge of envy) spacious balconies overlooking lush forests and sparkling lakes. These are the homes of year-round residents. If I lived here, you think to yourself. I'd have no complaints. But if you were to stick around and get acquainted with the people inside those homes, you'd find they face many of the same life challenges you do. And, yes, you'd hear plenty of them complain. While "location, location, location" has a lot to do with the value of real estate, it has little to do with thankfulness and contentment.

Thankfulness is a response not to the view outside your window, but to the view inside your heart. It begins with a Spirit-inspired appraisal of who you are: a living person experiencing with every breath the God-given miracle of life. In addition to the gift of your physical life, God has endowed you with a living soul so you can live year-round a fulfilling and exciting spiritual life. Then he fills the rooms of your soul with his Spirit so you can embrace all the benefits of a believing life, a life of faith in his words of forgiveness, trust in his promises, and assurance of salvation. A heart of gratitude for the wonder of life responds with thanksgiving in all places . . . in all circumstances . . . on all occasions. Because he has made you his daughter, his son, you're always looking out at a spectacular view of his eternal love and care.

Your home address has no effect on whether or not you're a thankful person. The location of your spirit has everything to do with your willingness and ability to give thanks. On the mountain-top, in the hills, or on the plains, give him your heartfelt thanks and praise!

Give thanks to the Lord, call on his name – make known among the nations what he has done.
1 CHRONICLES 16:8

Cultivate the thankful Spirit!
It will be to you a perpetual feast.
JOHN R. MACDUFF

Dear Father:

I ask you for so many things. My requests go on and on, but right now, at this moment, all I want to do is praise you. Please accept my thanks for all your great kindnesses, for life and love and peace and joy. Thank you for the remarkable nature of your journey to bring me back to you. I'm so glad you did.

Amen.

Row, Row, Row Your Boat

I consider that our present sufferings are not worth comparing with the glory that will be revealed in us.

ROMANS 8:18

A small lake lies below in the valley, and today you and your children have decided to row across to the other side. The outing begins well —everyone enthusiastic and eager to hit the water. But before they've even reached the midway point, your children are complaining. One whines, "I'm tired! My arms ache!" Another sighs, "Why do we have to keep doing this?" Though you encourage them to keep rowing until the boat reaches the opposite shore, they slam down their oars and declare, "You must hate us!"

Do you act like a child sometimes when you get tired of rowing through life? Perhaps you're in a trial that has worn you down so much you came to the mountains to escape it for a week or two. You've gone to the Lord and told him, "I'm tired!" Good. He understands. Many times throughout his ministry on earth he felt tired and needed rest. You might have complained, "My arms ache!" Good. He cares. He invites you to let him lift the weight of hardship from your shoulders. But when the trial gets long— when circumstances force you to keep rowing—you may well groan, "Why do I have to keep doing this?" and conclude. "God, you must hate me." Not so good.

Just as you, a loving parent, know what your children need to know about rowing — that giving up and turning back can cause you to miss out on all the amazing sights and sounds and fun that can be found on the other side of the lake — so God knows what you need to learn about life. He knows which spiritual muscles need toning, which skills need mastering, and he knows the benefits you will experience on the other side of the trial if you will only persevere. Though you're in deep water, keep rowing. Your heavenly Father knows what you can do and how long you can do it. And like a good parent, he's in the boat right now and showing you how.

> *Blessed is the man who perseveres under trial, because when he has stood the test, he will receive the crown of life that God has promised to those who love him.*
> *JAMES 1:12*

> *In shunning a trial we are seeking to avoid a blessing.*
> *CHARLES SPURGEON*

Dear Father:

Thank you for the wonderful rewards that wait on the other side of my trials. They inspire me to keep paddling until I reach peaceful shores. Thank you also for riding in the boat with me through every unfortunate circumstance. You are my comfort, my encouragement, and my guide.

Amen.

Path of Saints

*You will keep in perfect peace him whose mind is
steadfast, because he trusts in you. Trust in the Lord
forever, for the Lord, the Lord, is the Rock eternal.*

ISAIAH 26:3-4

Out for a walk along a mountain path, you come. A bridge spans the crevasse, but you hesitate to step onto it. The anchoring ropes look worn and frayed. Cracked foot boards and a broken handrail catch your eye. If you're smart, you won't trust the rickety bridge to get you safely to the other side.

God wants you to trust him, but he doesn't ask you to step onto a rickety spiritual bridge of uncertain strength. He gives you signs of his trustworthiness. First, he tells you in Scripture how he has come through for many who came before you. You have the testimony of King David, who trusted in God to save him from his enemies and fulfill his promise to make him king. You read about Peter's cry to Jesus and his trust in Christ to pull the floundering disciple out of deep water. You realize the extent of the apostle Paul's trust in God to deliver him through the hardships of his arduous ministry. Then, God shows you how he has come through for his present-day people. Talk with fellow believers and learn the many ways they have trusted God in both ordinary and extraordinary times. Living testimony attests to firm foot boards. Finally, God shows you how he will come through for you. He already has brought you through many trials. He promises you all things will work together for the good of you, his beloved child. He reaches out to you and invites you to hold on to him, to trust in his strength to get you across any deep ravine life has put or will ever put in your path. Personal experience confirms a reliable handrail.

Rely on God, who has proven worthy of your trust. Anchored in faith, hold firmly to him and walk confidently in the way of his saints who have gone before.

Blessed is the man who trusts in the Lord, whose confidence is in him. He will be like a tree planted by the water that sends out its roots by the stream. It does not fear when heat comes; its leaves are always green. It has no worries in a year of drought and never fails to bear fruit.
JEREMIAH 17:7-8

In God alone there is faithfulness and faith in the trust that we may hold to him, to his promise, and to his guidance. To hold to God is to rely on the fact that God is there for me, and to live in this certainty.
KARL BARTH

Heavenly Father:

I place my trust in you. I trust you to love and care for me, to keep your promises, to provide for me everything I really need. You have never let me down and I don't believe you ever will. You are completely worthy of my trust.

Amen.

One and Together

---

*Be united with other Christians. A wall with loose
brick is not good. The bricks must be cemented
together.*

CORRIE TEN BOOM

A long the path, you stop to consider a fir tree, pick up a pine cone, examine a cobweb in a cave, and pull a blossom from a crevice. Add to those treasures a snowy peak, a forested slope, a silvery lake, a valley wrapped in stillness. Placed under an infinite sky. warmed by the sun, and graced by the moon, all of these things come together as one in the wondrous miracle called nature.

No one element of nature resembles the other, or has the same function as the other. In the same way, no two believers in the kingdom of God look alike or serve the same purpose, God's kingdom embraces saints of towering public achievement right along with saints of modest private accomplishment. The work of one saint spreads the message of Jesus Christ around the world, while the work of another adorns a hidden comer of his kingdom. Even the worship of saints differs, from the open arms and joyful voices of vibrant praise to the folded hands and gentle whisper of heartfelt prayer. Placed under an eternal God, enlivened by his Spirit, and blessed by his love, all his saints come together as one in the wondrous miracle called the kingdom of God.

Would you like to look out the window tomorrow morning and find yourself surrounded by only mountain peaks—no slopes, no valleys? Or only pine cones—no bushes, no colorful blossoms? No matter how majestic the mountain peak or how precious the pine cone, each would be the poorer without the other. You admire nature because each element is unique, awesome, surprising, yet unified one with the other. God gave you unique gifts, abilities, insights, and opportunities to serve. He made you like no one else and for a purpose no one else can fill. Yet in your distinctiveness, you serve in unity with all the saints of past, present, and future in a wondrous miracle—the kingdom of Almighty God.

It was [God] who gave some to he apostles, some to be prophets, some to be evangelists, and some to be pastors and teachers, to prepare God's people for works of service, so that the body of Christ may be built up until we all reach unity in the faith and in the knowledge of the Son of God and become mature, attaining to the whole measure of the fullness of Christ.
EPHESIANS 4:11-13

Dear Lord:

Thank you for the miracle of diversity within your kingdom. Each person expresses your creative genius in a different and unique way. Help us to look upon our differences with joy rather than frustration. Give us an appreciation for each other. And Lord, start with me.

Amen.

Looking Ahead

Where there is no vision, the people perish.
PROVERBS 29:18 KJV

Unless you have a particular gift for inspirational leadership, you might not think of yourself as a visionary. But you are. A visionary is someone with both feet on the ground who can see the path to the future—and you can do that.

Today your feet are standing on a mountaintop or close to it. You see trees and creeks, hills and mountains all around you. You admire the sunrise and sunset, take pictures of the scenery, and delight in discoveries both small and great, if you were not a visionary, you would observe nothing more than what's readily apparent to your eyes from where you're standing now. That's why the Holy Spirit has given you the gift of vision. As a visionary, you see beyond the magnificence of creation to the power and majesty of the Creator. In his creation, you affirm his presence in all he has made, including his presence in you. In his presence, you see his guidance, care, forgiveness, and protection following you all the days of your life. Your spiritual vision allows you to glimpse the eternal future God has in mind for you—salvation and eternal life with him in heaven. You see the wisdom of God leading you there according to his will and at the pace he wants you to travel.

Whether your eyes take in the emerald beauty of a lush forest or the gray dinginess of a downtrodden city, your spiritual vision remains the same. You never have to ask, "Is this it? Is this all there is?" Because the answer is a resounding "No!" The Holy Spirit has made you a visionary, and you see far past your present circumstances, way beyond your current struggles. From where you're standing today, you can see and see clearly everlasting life in the future and God's eternal goodness with you every step on the path along the way.

With the eyes of your heart enlightened, you may know what is the hope to which he has called you, what are the riches of his glorious inheritance among the saints, and what is the immeasurable greatness of his power for us who believe, according to the working of his great power.
EPHESIANS 1: 18-19 NRSV

Vision is the art of seeing things that are invisible.
JONATHAN SWIFT

Dear Lord:

Open my eyes to see the spiritual goal you've set before me. Then I will keep my vision fixed, never surrendering to the obstacles in the path ahead. I trust you, Lord, not only to show me the purpose for my life but also to empower me to reach it.

Amen.

Read the Rules

The statutes of the Lord are trustworthy,
making wise the simple.
PSALM 19:7

O n this day, you've chosen to visit a nearby national park. You're looking forward to seeing some animals unique to the area. But before you see anything else, you notice a posted list of rules and warnings. Rangers post this information about potential danger from animals, insects, fire, or falling rocks. You read that a rogue bear has been spotted in the area and you should never carry food with you. You also read that a drought is in progress. Dry timber can lead to fires, so you should build a campfire only in specially designated spots. To enjoy your visit and use the area safely and responsibly, you need to acknowledge these warnings and rules. You ignore the warnings and break the rules at your own peril and the peril of others.

When God reveals facts that challenge human thinking, some people shut their ears to them. People want to have a good time without the limitations of living by God's rules. But God gave his commandments and made known his will not to put a damper on life, but to allow his people to delight in life and live in his world safely and responsibly. He know's the effects of sin, and he wants you to avoid sin so you don't suffer its destructive consequences or harm others. He posts his rules and warnings in front of you and sends you his Spirit so you know the facts — the pleasant truths as well as the unpleasant ones. The truths that make you feel comfortable and the truths that make you squirm. The truths your friends agree with and the truths they ridicule you for taking seriously.

If you're heeding the rules and warnings in the park, you are a wise camper, indeed! And if you're heeding God's commandments and his will for your life, hooray! You are indeed a wise person.

Wisdom is as good as an inheritance, an advantage to those who see the sun. For the protection of wisdom is like the protection of money, and the advantage of knowledge is that wisdom gives life to the one who possesses it.
ECCLESIASTES 7:11-12 NRSV

One can have knowledge without having wisdom, but one cannot have wisdom without having knowledge.
R. C. SPROUL

Dear Lord:

Give me the wisdom to live within the perimeters you have set in your Word. I trust that you have my best interests at heart. Forgive me for the times I've stepped outside your boundaries and heal the hurts that resulted from those trespasses. I delight in following your commands.

Amen.

Expect and Get a Miracle

Come, let us bow down in worship,
let us kneel before the Lord our Maker.
PSALM 95:6

If you expect to get anything out of your vacation, you need to put something into it. if you expect to fish, you need to take your tackle to the water, if you expect to hike, you need to lace up your hiking shoes and get down to the trail, if you expect to roast marshmallows, you need to stoke the campfire. Many Christians, however, expect to get some thing out of worship without putting anything into it.

God promises his presence when believers gather together in the name of Jesus Christ. When you assemble with others in church for worship, you can and should expect God's presence. And you have it. God's presence means he's doing things. Through readings, preaching, singing, anthems, and sacraments, he's reaching out to you and serving you with his wisdom and strength, his correction, counsel, and comfort. But if you expect to get anything out of his words to you, you need to take your ears to the sanctuary. If you expect to gain more understanding into his will for your life, you need to focus your attention on what he's telling you. Worship time is no time for mental multitasking. Your divided heart, your wandering thoughts, cannot expect—and w'ill not get—the full counsel of God offers to you in worship. Put yourself into worship and you will get great things in return. You will get God, who in Jesus Christ gave himself to you. You will go home with the rich blessings and powerful benefits he wants to give you when you come to worship him.

God is present in worship, but forces himself on no one, Rather, he invites you to give him your willing obedience, your mindful attention, and your humble heart. When you put those things into your worship, you can expect—and get —a miracle.

Ascribe to the Lord the glory due his name;
worship the Lord in the splendor of his holiness.
P S A L M 2 9 : 2

The perfect church service would be one we were
almost unaware of; our attention would have
been on God.
C. S. L E W I S

Heavenly Father:

My desire is to worship you – in word, in deed, and in truth. Teach
me to do so in a way that's pleasing to you – a way that allows me
to leave everything else behind and focus completely on your love,
your goodness, your peace, your joy.

Amen.

On the Heights with Jesus

*We pray that if any, anywhere, are fearing that
the cost of discipleship is too great, that they may
be given to glimpse that treasure in heaven.*
ELISABETH ELLIOT

Gazing out at the mountains from the deck of your secluded cabin, your eyes fall on a huge, distant, icy summit. How impossible that ascent appears.

Why do people climb mountains? Only those dedicated climbers who get a taste of it and cannot get enough of the challenge can really come close to understanding the compulsion. And even they are unable to find the words to explain it. They just can't *not do it.*

That's how following Jesus seems. It can be rough, difficult — an uphill struggle. Yet to the disciple compelled by love, the question is, "How much do I love the one who is calling me upward, and is there anything I would not do to be near him?"

You imagine Jesus standing confidently on the top of that mountain. "Come! Follow me!" he shouts with a smile, and tosses down a rope. Your heart answers yes, even as it pounds with fear.

The reward of discipleship, according to theologian Dallas Willard, is "abiding peace, a life penetrated throughout by love, faith that sees everything in the light of

God's over-riding governance for good, hopefulness that stands firm in the most discouraging of circumstances, power to do what is right and withstand the forces of evil . . . that abundance of life Jesus said he came to bring."

And Jesus will never let you walk alone. Though your path may wind through rugged terrain and dizzying heights, he is there to help you, provide living water for your journey, infuse you with his strength, encourage, and sustain you.

After all, he's been up the steepest passages himself and is more than able to take you there.

> *[Jesus said,] "Remain in me, and I will remain in you. No branch can bear fruit by itself, it must remain in the vine. Neither can you bear fruit unless you remain in me. I am the vine; you are the branches. If a man remains in me and I in him, he will bear much fruit; apart from me you can do nothing."*
> *JOHN 15:4-5*

Dear Father:

I want to be your true disciple — the kind that follows you up the side of a mountain if necessary, the kind that never lets you out of their sight, the kind that can do nothing less than serve you completely. What I desire to do, I cannot do on my own. Help me, Lord, to be your disciple.

Amen.

Avoiding a Fall

Therefore encourage one another and build each
other up, just as in fact you are doing.
1 THESSALONIANS 5:11

A sk any serious mountaineer: solo climbing is dangerous business. The adventurous sense of freedom you first experience in setting off alone, unrestricted, can quickly turn to regret if you find yourself in a precarious position on the heights, minus the security of being roped to a companion. Of course, not just any companion will do; wise climbers know the importance of choosing someone reliable, whose skill level matches their own. If one of you makes a foolish move at 2,000 feet, you both have a long way to fall!

In the same way, the companions we choose in our Christian walk can be a great help to us, or they Can drag us down. Spending a lot of time with someone who has a negative attitude or a destructive tongue tugs at the spirit like a heavy weight. The Bible warns against being "unequally yoked" with unbelievers.

Spending time with those who lift us up with their encouragement, however, can provide the security we need to enjoy the climb. Find those people who will say, "You can do it. I'm there for you. I'm praying. Keep your eyes on the goal. You've got it now. You're doing great!" The Christian walk is a serious climb with dangers all along the way. Be sure you are tied to someone who will help you get there. Form close connections over time with people who consistently encourage you and challenge you to live a holy life. Then, as trust increases, so will vulnerability.

God designed us to function together, not alone. Don't be afraid to reach out for help—and for prayer—when you need it.

Let the word of Christ dwell in you richly as you teach and admonish one another with all wisdom, and as you sing psalms, hymns, and spiritual songs with gratitude in your hearts to God.
COLOSSIANS 3:16

One of the highest of human duties is the duty of encouragement.
WILLIAM BARCLAY

Lord God:

Send encouragers into my life – those who will lift me up in my Christian walk. Help me always to encourage others as well, to be the kind of person who offers a word or deed at just the right time. Thank you for not leaving me to do a "solo climb" but for providing me with good companions.

Amen.

Taking in the View

*This is the testimony: God has given us eternal
life, and this life is in his Son. He who has the
Son has life; he who does not have the Son of God
does not have life.*
1 JOHN 5:11-12

It's surprising how you can limit your own perspective at times. Worries and concerns can so easily cause you to see only what is directly in front of you. It's as if God is offering to show you the vista from a ski lift high in the Alps, but instead you crouch, with eyes downcast, on a hill the size of a pitcher's mound!

It can be hard to grasp the truth that this life on earth is incredibly brief compared to eternity—like a mist, or a wildflower that blooms for a little while and is gone. The finite mind cannot understand eternity! And how can you ever begin to glimpse its enormity when your circumstances tie you to the ordinary, day-to-day events right around you?

An amazing transformation can take place within you, when you allow your Father's arms to lift you to the heights for a better view. Suddenly you feel both very small and very safe at the same time. You realize that the few years we are given on this earth must certainly be very precious to him: you want to know the purpose he's laid out for your life, once you see your existence for the brief, exquisite flash of light that it is.

"I lift my eyes up to the mountains," says the psalmist.

Lift up your eyes from the "boulders" that stand as obstacles before you, and look to the endless peaks beyond. Take in the vastness of God's creation as a reminder that he is himself vast beyond your imagining.

Be encouraged, when problems seem to block your spiritual vision. God sees and knows all, and he cares about you deeply. His promises and blessings are not just for this life — but life eternal!

The one who sows to please the Spirit, from the Spirit will reap eternal life. Let us not become weary in doing good, for at the proper time we will reap a harvest if we do not give up.
GALATIANS 6:8-9

Eternal life does not begin with death; it begins with faith.
SAMUEL M. SHOEMAKER

Heavenly Father:

I can hardly imagine spending eternity with you. It's one of those things that I believe but cannot grasp. You might say it's a promise too great for me. Teach me to live my life in light of eternity, for it is only then that I can see my life here as it truly is — endless.

Amen.

Don't Look Down!

*Be on your guard; stand firm in the faith;
be men of courage; be strong.*
1 CORINTHIANS 16:13

If you've ever been a novice at rappelling, you are no doubt familiar with the tingly, stomach-flip-flopping thrill of backing off a cliff for the first time. You know you're safe because your guide has amply demonstrated the flawless ropes and hardware that are holding you. You wouldn't be there if you didn't trust that little makeshift nylon "car seat."

You probably watched several others go before you — unless you're the brave, reckless soul who volunteered, "Me first!" Out they swing, and back they spring, sliding gracefully down on what appears, from a distance, no more than a swaying strand. Oh, but they're having a blast!

Still . . . it's that moment when you have to walk backward into space, and *every* instinct that has kept you alive till this point rebels against the thought! You feel frozen at the edge. Your rappelling companions gently urge you, and you feel a little foolish for holding up the line.

Finally, you close your eyes tightly and take the plunge; that's when the fun begins!

Our faith walk can be much the same way. Even though we read the Bible and believe we can take God at his word, our feelings sometimes take a little while to snap into place with our faith.

No need to worry. Some are impetuous, like Peter, and jump out of the boat to walk on water with the Lord. Others are a little more reticent, like Thomas, who needed to touch and see Jesus' wounds before accepting that he was the risen Lord. But God knows us all intimately and works with us right where we are. He understands that "backing off" feeling very well. What counts is where your faith walk ultimately takes you once you've overcome the initial jitters!

Take courage, and let your faith guide you into his great adventure.

Trust in the Lord forever, for in the Lord God
you have an everlasting rock
ISAIAH 26:4 NRSV

Reason is an action of the mind; knowledge is a
possession of the mind; but faith is an attitude of
the person. It means you are prepared to stake
yourself on something being so.
MICHAEL RAMSEY

Dear Lord:

Thank you for the great adventure of following you through my life. Even though sometimes I look at my circumstances and feel a twinge of anxiety, still I know that I have no reason to fear, for my rope is securely fastened to yours and you will never let me fall.

Amen.

Linked by a Calling

I choose as my friends everyone who worships
you and follows your teachings.
P S A L M   1 1 9 : 6 3   C E V

The mountains are calling. You heard them and were drawn here from your home. Others heard them as well, from miles in the other direction, and so they came. Maybe friendship was already established, and this adventure is a project you have been planning for a while. Or maybe you've only recently become acquainted. Maybe it's only the mountains that you have in common. But you've decided to set off together, linked by your love of these hills and your shared excitement over the quest ahead.

Gear is packed and ready; bodies are rested and eager. It's only the inception of your journey, yet you feel strangely close to these companions. After all, hiking up steep, rocky terrain isn't just everyone's idea of fun. But to you and to these kindred souls, the thrill of this experience is well worth the hard work and preparation—and yes, even the danger. Having the same enthusiasm for climbing would, by itself, explain why you feel especially bonded.

Yet something else enhances your ties: the lofty goal ahead of you! You're heading for the same summit, with the quiet understanding that if one stumbles or tires, another will be there to support him.

That's how it is with the Christian life. God, in his great love, has given us a whole variety of fellow "climbers" with whom to link hearts and share the journey. Those you feel closest to in this life are those who, like you, have heard that irresistible call beckoning them to a higher place—a more meaningful way to walk out these few days here on earth. You want to be with people who feel the same passion you do. You know how important their support is in a world that's not always kind to our dreams.

Be grateful for your fellow climbers! See them as the gift they are, and thank your Creator for them. Your truest Friend has given you the gift of friendship.

Some friends play at friendship but a true friend
sticks closer than one's nearest kin.
PROVERBS 18:24 NKSV

Friendship is one of the sweetest joys of life.
Many might have failed beneath the bitterness of
their trial had they not found a friend.
CHARLES SPURGEON

Dear Father:

Thank you for friends of like mind to accompany me on my journey of faith. They bring me encouragement and comfort as I strive to accomplish the tasks you've set before me. Show me how to be a good friend to them as well – a caring, encouraging, loving friend.

Amen.

Irretrievably Gone

*I, even I, am he who blots out your transgressions, for
my own sake, and remembers your sins no more.*
ISAIAH 43:25

High on a sun-drenched ledge, you lean back and feel the breeze softly cooling your skin. With a deep, contented breath of mountain air, you survey the lovely, over-the-treetops view.

A small stone, just the right size for throwing, sits just within arm's reach. You lazily pick it up and watch transfixed, as your fist sends it sailing over the edge, down, down, to disappear far below. You do not see it reach the ground.

Think about God's forgiveness and how he assures us that he separates us far from our sinful deeds once we have confessed them. "As far as the east is from the west" —so far we cannot imagine retrieving them, any more than you can imagine retrieving that disappearing stone you just cast off the mountain.

The concept of forgiveness is all about casting off. In the original language, the idea of yielding up and casting off is central.

Your past sins need never become your identity. You are what you become from this moment forward. Satan, the Accuser, will try to tell you that your sins are not really gone; that their shadow will always hang over you. His lies can be very convincing, because we feel bad about the wrong things we have done and find it hard, sometimes to believe God could really cast them away so far that they are forgotten! But don't allow doubts and self-destructive suggestions to invade your mind, if God says you are truly forgiven, then you are.

Remind yourself of the permanence of his forgiveness. In your mind's eye, return to that cliff whenever you are tempted to hold on to past sins. Pick up a stone, wind up, and hurl it as far as you can throw it into the thick, distant treetops. Is there any way you could find it after that? Why would you ever want to try?

> *[The Lord] does not deal with us according to our sins,*
> *nor repay us according to our iniquities. For as the*
> *heavens are high above the earth, so great is his*
> *steadfast love towards those who fear him, as far as the*
> *east is from the west, so far he removes our*
> *transgressions from us.*
> *PSALM 103:10-12 NRSV*

> *God does not wish us to remember*
> *what he is willing to forget.*
> *GEORGE ARTHUR BUTTRICK*

Dear Lord:

How wonderful it feels to know that I am forgiven — all my sins, all my guilt gone for good. I know that forgiveness is possible only because of Jesus' sacrifice on the cross. It was a price I cannot comprehend, but one I will always appreciate with my entire heart and soul.

Amen.

On Eagles' Wings

*Now that you have been set free from sin and have
become slaves to God, the benefit you reap leads to
holiness, and the result is eternal life.*

ROMANS 6:22

In the open mountain air, you stand and look up at the clean expanse overhead. You cannot believe how blue the sky is — strikingly, vividly blue against the peaks, without a cloud in sight. Suddenly into your field of vision soars an eagle. Wings spread majestically, held aloft on Invisible air currents — what an incredible sight to behold! Could any living creature appear more free and confident? Is there any more beautiful picture of strength and grace combined?

An eagle in flight is so stately, so unfettered. Long, broad wings and fanned tail are held strong and stiff, enabling the eagle to glide great distances while the air flows smoothly over their surface. Their size and shape enable them to easily support the eagle's heavy body as it freely maneuvers the skies.

Yet on the ground, these same wings and tail appear clumsy. Suddenly you are watching a very different sort of creature: an earthbound, oversized bird in a graceless struggle with gravity.

Your liberty in Christ is like that. It is a gift of your wise Creator, whose Word tells you just how you ought to handle it — not as freedom *to* sin. but as freedom *from* sin. Guided by righteousness and held aloft by God's grace and strength, you find yourself able to maneuver life's turbulent times. But let sin and unbelief weigh you down, and what started out as liberty becomes awkward and heavy.

Golden eagles make their nests high on remote cliffs in the mountains. They hunt in daylight, and at night keep themselves safe in their aeries or on a secure perch. As a Christian, your safety is ensured by staying close to Jesus, your high tower. And your freedom is in following his ways, walking not in darkness but soaring in his light, far above the cares of this world.

To him who loves us and has freed us from our sins by his blood, and has made us to be a kingdom and priests to serve his God and Father — to him be glory and power for ever and ever!
REVELATION 1:5-6

Freedom means I have been set free to become all that God wants me to be, to achieve all that God wants me to achieve, to enjoy all that God wants me to enjoy.
WARREN W. WIERSBE

Heavenly Father:

It's such an exhilarating feeling to be free — free to choose to live my life with you. No longer shackled by the weight of sin. I can be all that you've created me to be. Thank you for giving me the greatest gift of all: the choice to love and serve you.

Amen.

Created for Closeness

The Lord is with you, while you are with him. If
you seek him, he will be found by you.
2 CHRONICLES 15:2 NRSV

Why is it that God seems so much more easily accessible in nature? You sense his nearness when surrounded by the beauty of the things he made. You hear his gentle voice in the wind and catch a glimpse of his radiance when you see sunlight glint on dew-drenched grass. The enormous variety of interesting animal species vividly reminds you of his incredible creativity. And the strong forces that formed the mountains and valleys are clear evidence that God is much bigger and more powerful than we can imagine.

The Bible says that creation speaks without words. It gives testimony to the one who placed the stars in the sky and taught the eagle how to fly.

But God is not only found inglorious sunsets and mountain vistas. In fact, there is nowhere you can go where his Spirit is not. Most important of all, you must know him in the secret place: your own heart.

While the world is God's showcase, the human heart is his intimate chamber. It's the place where he desires to be invited and stay, as your dear, trusted companion.

Take him in with all your senses. Listen to the many different ways he communicates when ears are open and eager to hear his voice. At the sight of a distant, jagged mountain range shouting, "God is holy!" be filled with awe.

As your bare feet walk, across a mountain stream, let the touch of velvet moss on smooth stones whisper to you the mysteries of his comfort and endless mercy. Walk closely with him and hear his voice of loving instruction wherever you go. Know and worship him as both the amazing, peerless God of the universe . . . and the friend who sticks closer than a brother.

"You will call upon me and come and pray to me, and I will listen to you. You will seek me and find me when you seek me with all your heart. I will be found by you," declares the Lord.
JEREMIAH 29:12 – 14

So necessary is our friendship to God that he approaches us and asks us to be his friends.
MEISTER ECKHART

Dear Father:

I revel in the wonder of being your child – but to be your friend? I can hardly comprehend it. Show me how to walk worthy of such a friendship – to be allowed into your presence without hesitation, to serve your purposes here on earth, to carry your message to others. What a wonderful gift.

Amen.

Sweet Song of Sacrifice

*A generous man will prosper, he who refreshes
others will himself be refreshed.*
Proverbs 11:25

Y ou hear the little mountain stream long before
you see it. Its light, bubbly chatter reminds you
of a group of excited children busy at play, or a
happily nervous choral ensemble warming up for their big
performance with rapid up-and-down scales.

The water running over smooth, round, multi-colored
pebbles reflects quick flashes of bright sunlight, adding to its
air of giddy celebration. You just *feel* the joy here, as though
each droplet is a single note added to a chorus of delight—
delight in what? In bounding down over the rugged stones
to join in the river that rushes all the way down to the
valleys from melting-snow-topped peaks above.

This is the picture painted by Hannah Hurnard in her
allegory *Hinds' Feet on High Places.* She writes about the song
sung by the rushing water: an expression of pure joy. The joy,
she says, results from the excitement the water feels upon
leaving the highest heights for the lowest places, in order to
serve the needs of those in the valley. She compares their
song of sacrifice to the pure joy a Christian experiences in
leaving a mountaintop encounter with God to fulfill his

command to bring Jesus into the lives of those who so desperately need him.

It is wonderful to draw close to God and have quiet times alone with him, seeking wisdom and spiritual revelation.But giving is what your heart and hands were made for. You will find no greater satisfaction than that of using what God has given you to show love toward others. Jesus is the Living Water, a never-ending supply for those who come to him. When you have tasted of him, go where he sends you to share that life-giving, thirst-quenching gift! Water the valleys with his love. Hear the song your heart sings when it knows the true joy of giving.

Jesus himself said: "It is more blessed to give
than to receive."
A C T S 2 0 : 3 5

You are never more like God than when you give.
A U T H O R U N K N O W N

Dear Father:

You have given so much to me. I desire to give to others from my abundance. Whisper to me when there is a need I am able to fill — whether that should be a financial gift, a smile, a kind word, a helping hand. What I give to others will always be just a small expression of your kindness and generosity to me.

Amen.

Protective Headgear

*So let us put aside the deeds of darkness
and put on the armor of light.*
ROMANS 13:12

The mountains stand so still and quiet. You stand still, also silent, taking in their great size and stature. Impressed with the massive stability of these unshakable rocks, you are speechless with awe.

Suddenly your reverie is interrupted by the distant, thunderous clatter of stones. You see them now, careening down the mountainside—luckily, not near where you are standing, unshakable? Maybe not!

Falling rocks are one of the major causes of death or serious head injury to the rock climber. In spite of this, many prefer to climb without a helmet, exposing themselves to real danger. It's surprising, that so many don't protect themselves with proper headgear.

The apostle Paul warns Christians that they need to put on the full armor of God, including the "helmet of salvation." We need these items, he writes in his letter to the Ephesians, in order to stand firm against the schemes of the Devil. Not only does Satan continually hurl "stones" of doubt and unbelief our way, he also uses other people to shake our faith.

Many times rocks are dislodged by other climbers rather than by the unassisted force of gravity. The climber wears a helmet, in this case, to keep safe from the destructive influence of others.

We live in a world filled with destructive influences. As you make the journey — often a difficult, upward climb — it's important to be secure in the salvation Jesus bought for you with his life.

You must arm your mind with his peace and assurance; you must rest in his love at all times and not give place in your thoughts to worry or anxiety. Trust in God can protect your mind in the same way that a physical helmet protects you outwardly. Nothing can penetrate a firm belief in God's goodness. Wear it at all times!

Be strong in the Lord and in his mighty power.
Put on the full armor of God so that you can take
your stand against the devil's schemes.
EPHESIANS 6:10-11

Security is not the absence of danger, but the
presence of God, no matter what the danger.
AUTHOR UNKNOWN

Heavenly Father:

Thank you for giving me the tools I need to protect myself from my spiritual enemies. I resolve not to give heed to the fiery darts they throw my way. Instead I will put my faith in you and in your Word that I might walk safely through this life.

Amen.

Certified Mountain Movers

*Ah Lord God! It is you who made the heavens
and the earth by your great power and by your
outstretched arm! Nothing is too hard for you.*
JEREMIAH 32:17 NRSV

Everyone knows the mountains are huge. When seen from a distance, they are beautifully impressive. But now, here you are, up close and personal, and you are blown away by the power they silently exert over the landscape. You don't know when you have ever felt so small.

You search for adjectives to describe what you are seeing. "Big" and "heavy" seem ridiculously inadequate. Enormous? Gigantic? Massive? A little better. But the word that keeps repeating itself to you is "immovable. " Nothing could budge these things. No way.

Then you recall what Jesus had to say about mountains and the faith to move them. He told his followers that with faith the size of a tiny mustard seed, they had the authority to say to a mountain, "Get up and jump into the sea." And it would obey!

Only Christ has that kind of authority over nature, and isn't it amazing that he passes his authority on to his people? Believe in him, and there's nothing you can't do, when you pray according to his will.

Now, it's rare that Jesus prompts one to defy laws of nature in such a dramatic way as physically moving mountains. But he can and may lead you to pray for seemingly impossible obstacles to be removed. He delights in your obedience when you take the authority he's granted you and use it boldly to see his miracles transform lives and circumstances.

A soldier once came to Jesus because his servant was very ill. He told Jesus that, being himself a man under authority, he understood that all Jesus had to do was say the word, and the servant would be well. Jesus approved of his faith and healed the man. That soldier clearly understood the power of authority.

Mountains may seem huge and immovable, but to the one who created them, they are no more than pebbles. See the mountains standing in your way with eyes of faith.

Our prayers lay the track down on which God's power can come. Like a mighty locomotive, his power is irresistible, but it cannot reach us without rails.
WATCHMAN NEE

Dear Father:

Teach me to use the authority you've given me to move the mountains in my life and the lives of those I love. I am an eager student, not because I long to be powerful, but because I love to extend your hand of healing and deliverance to others.

Amen.

Unplugged and Still Listening

What's the price of a pet canary? Some loose change,
right? And God cares what happens to it even more
than you do. He pays even greater attention to you.
down to the last detail — even numbering the hairs on
your head! So don't be intimidated by all this bully
talk. You're worth more than a million canaries.
MATTHEW 10:29-31 MSG

Ah, the joy of being free form distractions. You haven't watched TV for several days. The telephone doesn't ring, because you're way out of range! No traffic, no noisy neighbors, no interruptions. Just a whole lot of time to relax and enjoy this remote mountain vacation.

Still, every now and then you feel uneasy. Why? Maybe it's because — even though you know you don't want to — if you did decide to rejoin civilization, it would take quite some time to get there. Being this far from the busy world you are used to is both heavenly . . . and a little disconcerting.

At times like this, you realize your vulnerability. It becomes clearer to you how much we have come to depend on one another and the conveniences on which we've come to rely. From knowing you can pick up the phone and order a pizza, to the assurance that dialing 9-1-1 will bring the help you need in an emergency, there are advantages to staying connected.

But to the one who trusts in Jesus, it's comforting to know that the Lord never sleeps. He watches over you night and day, alone or in a crowd. You are never outside the boundaries of his care.

When the psalmist David was hiding from evil men seeking his life, he demonstrated faith in God's constant care: "But you are a shield around me. O Lord; you bestow glory on me and lift up my head. I lie down and sleep; I wake again, because the Lord sustains me. I will not fear the tens of thousands drawn up against me on every side" (Ps. 3:3, 5-6).

How sweet to have such confidence in the God who loves you. Remember, he watches over you every minute. Just lift up your eyes and ask, "Lord . . . can you hear me now?" He can.

The Lord my pasture shall prepare, and feed me
with a shepherd's care; his presence shall my
wants supply, and guard me with a watchful eye.
JOSEPH ADDISON

Heavenly Father:

You are always watching — I believe that with all my heart. I lie down at night and sleep because I know you are looking after me and I have nothing to fear. Thank you for your gracious, loving care. It sustains me wherever I go.

Amen.

Always More to Discover

*Daniel said: "Blessed be the name of God from
age to age. for wisdom and power are his. He
changes times and seasons, deposes kings and
sets up kings: he gives wisdom to the wise and
knowledge to those who have understanding. He
reveals deep and hidden things: he knows what is
in the darkness, and light dwells with him. To
you, O God of my ancestors. I give thanks and
praise, for you have given me wisdom and power
and have now revealed to me what we asked of
you."*
DANIEL 2:20-23 NRSV

Nothing seems as unchanging as the broad, majestic mountains. Still, after spending some time here, tucked away so near them, you realize you are just beginning to get to know them. You're discovering there are as many subtle facets to this range as there are to an old and dear friend. The now-familiar silhouette of their unique shape never changes, but the ridges and crevices on their faces reveal a wide variety of personalities, depending on the time of day, the weather, and the season.

What marvels of creation they are. They remind you of the beauty and complexity of the character of God. His Word teaches that while he is the same yesterday, today and forever, there is so much to know of his ways and his character that you could spend a lifetime seeking him and only scratch the surface.

The more you get to know God. the deeper you will want to explore his wisdom. The better you understand his holiness, the greater your desire will be to spend time with him in order to become more like him. There's nothing more exciting than those rare moments when you catch a glimpse of him in you! God is total beauty, utter perfection. Getting to know him is an adventure that never becomes tiresome, because he is more fascinating than any wonder of nature — even these incredible, changing yet unchanging hills.

The attributes of God, though intelligible to us on their surface yet, for the very reason that they are infinite, transcend our comprehension, when they are dwelt upon, when they are followed out, and can only be received by faith.
CARDINAL JOHN HENRY NEWMAN

Dear Father:

I want to know you better and better each day. even though I know even in eternity I will never know you completely. You are too great and mighty for me. And yet, you have asked me to prove your character — your faithfulness, love, and goodness. Thank you for stooping down and allowing me to know you.

Amen.

Never failing, Never false

*The Lord is faithful to all his promises and loving
toward all he has made.*
P S A L M   1 4 5 : 1 3

How do you know when you've reached the top of a mountain?

The question about what constitutes an official peak has long been a topic of debate among mountaineers. Most of them know all about the disappointment of reaching a "false summit." When you achieve what you think is the summit and discover that the peak you are trying to climb is still farther and higher, you are on a false summit.

Who hasn't experienced something similar on a personal level? You aim your hopes and expectations toward a desired goal—or a certain person—only to discover that your confidence was misplaced. The someone or something you thought might hold the answer to your problems eventually proves false. Your trust was misplaced, and you have to turn elsewhere.

Aren't you glad this cannot happen with God? He gives his word that he is exactly who he says he is. The only surprises with the Lord are good surprises! When you put your faith in him and follow him, you are continually blessed to find that he not only meets but exceeds your expectations.

God does not lead you on with false hope. He will take you by the hand and guide you, fulfilling every promise he has made— and then some. It's true that your path with him may not always take you to the exact place you had envisioned, but that is only because his own vision is so much higher and better.

If you feel you have put your faith in God yet reached a "false summit," it is usually because your vision was not set high enough in the first place. His plans for you are far greater than you might imagine, and it is sometimes hard to grasp just how wonderful a future he really has in store for those who love him. Believe in your awesome God and his faithfulness. He will not disappoint you.

Know therefore that the Lord your God is God; he is the faithful God, keeping his covenant of love to a thousand generations of those who love him and keep his commands.
DEUTERONOMY 7:9

What more powerful consideration can be thought on to make us true to God, than the faithfulness and truth of God to us?
WILLIAM GURNALL

Heavenly Father:

I am ever grateful for your faithfulness. I count it an honor to follow you and you alone, for you never fail – ever! You always accomplish what you have set out to do. You keep every promise – every one. Your wisdom and power are indisputable – never wavering.

Amen.

A Broad Place to Stand

From the fullness of his grace we have all
received one blessing after another.
JOHN 1:16

Glad to be out of the vehicle and on your two feet again, feeling the thinness of the air at this altitude, and just a bit wobbly in the knees front the harrowing ride around hairpin turns up this steep mountain road . . . you inhale deeply and look around for a place to sit down and rest.

Thank you, Lord! The terrain opens up onto a broad, open plateau. It is refreshing to stand on wide, level ground again. It helps you relax and get back to the mind set of enjoying this breathtaking view. You are able to look around you and take in the beauty from a whole new height. You feel captured by joy, just to be here and feel this incredible freedom.

The psalmist David, thankful to God for his great care, wrote, "You . . . set my feet in a spacious place" (Ps. 34:8).

Grace is such a very spacious place. You may come close to slipping and falling more often than you care to admit, but again and again the Lord preserves you—setting your feet on a spacious place. He could require you to balance on a narrow ledge of rigid obedience, but he doesn't, even though he has every right to hold you to his standard of holiness. But Jesus chose to give his life, and in so doing, bought your acceptance into eternity and gave you a way to live by grace instead.

Love of Christ makes you want to do right, and his Spirit empowers you to press on toward that goal. But your dear Friend is always there to relieve you when the way gets steep and difficult. When you are weak, he sets you down on an open plain to help you get your bearings once again and give you the strength to keep moving upward.

God is able to make all grace abound to you, so that in all things at all times, having all that you need, you will abound in every good work.
2 CORINTHIANS 9:8

There is nothing but God's grace. We walk upon it; we breathe it; we live and die by it; it makes the nails and axles of the universe.
ROBERT LOUIS STEVENSON

Oh Holy Father:

I don't deserve your grace. It is certainly unmerited. But I do accept the grace you pour out on me — grace that I receive because of the sacrifice of your pure and flawless Son, Jesus. What an indescribable gift!

Amen.

Your Creator's Calling Card

How great is the love the Father has lavished on us, that we should be called children of God! And that is what we are!

1 JOHN 3:1

A lone on the gently sloping expanse of a mountain meadow, you scan the rich array of wild- flowers that carpet the hillsides. How tender God is with his creation, how attentive to the smallest artistic detail. Buttery yellow daisies, delicate blue columbine, and bold red-orange poppies pose together in a gorgeous splash of color. What food for the eyes! What a well-chosen palette the Artist uses, yet how uninhibited is his selection of colors!

Why does God take such great care with everything he places in nature—even these small, fragrant gems who reign so briefly and are seen by so few? This scene and color scheme will soon change as one short season replaces another, and a whole new cast of flowers will fill the stage. Why is he so generous, so abundant in his giving? What compels him to create so beautifully, so thoughtfully, so tirelessly?

Is the answer as simple as "love"? Is God so full of love that he cannot go anywhere without making it beautiful? Does love splash and spill wherever he walks, and leave this kind of beauty in its wake?

What is the purpose of beauty? This fireworks display of wild flowers, the fascinating symphony songs of birds, the eye-catching flash of butterfly . . . did he leave them all here as a kind of "calling card"?

Perhaps God created this beauty just for you, just to catch your eye, just to let you know that he is there.

Stand very still in the thick, green grass and you can almost hear your Creator whisper, "I was here . . . do you recognize my work? I did it for you, because I love you and I want you to know me." Follow beauty to its source; it leads straight to your Father's heart of love.

You created my inmost being; you knit me
together in my mother's womb. I praise you
because I am fearfully and wonderfully made;
your works are wonderful. I know that full well.
PSALM 139:13-14

God's love for us is proclaimed with each
mountainscape.
AUTHOR UNKNOWN

Oh Dear Father:

I look around me and I am enraptured by what I see — your handiwork in the sunrise, in the starry sky, in the profusion of daffodils and elegant orange canna lilies. You are visible in every miracle of nature. Thank you for your loving touch on all the earth.

Amen.

Supreme in Power and in Love

His divine power has given us everything we need for
life and godliness through our knowledge of him who
called us by his own glory and goodness.
2 PETER 1:3

What began as a sunny hike on a mountain footpath has brought you to a higher elevation, past the lush greener of the tree line. You have entered a darkened crevasse between two towering, stony sentinels. The tall walls and stark grandeur of the barren rock put you in mind of an ancient castle or cathedral.

There is a strength in the mountains that causes you to feel small and humbled, as if in the presence of royalty. No surprise, then, that the terminology used to describe and measure some of the mountains' physical characteristics is regal-sounding.

For instance, a "monarch" is the highest peak in a group or range; a peak is considered "sovereign" if it stands alone has no neighbor inside its extent); and what is known as a peak's "power" is a calculation used to rank peaks against one another.

While scientists compare one mountain's size, scope, and altitude with another's, Psalm 97:5 puts it all in perspective in stating, "The mountains melt like wax before the Lord." Who is sovereign? Who has all the real power? Whose hand formed these spectacular specimens of nature?

The Lord over all the earth. The King above every earthly king. The one with whose power no man or phenomenon of nature can begin to compete.

Isn't it amazing just to think on his true power—and then to realize that this same Lord, who reigns supreme over all humankind and nature, loves you so very much?

Lord, you are great and powerful. Glory, majesty and beauty belong to you. Everything in heaven and on earth belongs to you. Lord, the kingdom belongs to you. You are honored as the One who rules over all. Wealth and honor come from you. You are the ruler of all things. In your hands are strength and power. You can give honor and strength to everyone.

1 CHRONICLES 29:11-12 NIRV

The greatest single distinguishing feature of the omnipotence of God us that our imagination gets lost thinking about it.

BLAISE PASCAL

Dear Lord:

I have no power but your power, no hope but your hope, no love but your love, no peace but your peace. You are everything to me and always will be. I feel no need. I am happy and secure. Keep me always close to your side where my heart can always be strengthened and filled.

Amen.

The Eloquence of Silence

"Be still, and know that I am God, "
[says the Lord Almighty.]
P S A L M   4 6 : 1 0

Y ou pitch your tent in the mountains on a beautiful, starlit evening. Lying on your back under the glittering expanse of night sky, you watch the dark become darker yet. Diamond-like points of light against the now inky-black velvet appear to multiply and become more brilliant by the minute. How silently yet how eloquently God speaks through his heavens.

Sometimes when you spend time with a close friend, no words are necessary—just being together is enough. It's been called "presencing." You derive something deeply needed, deeply nourishing, from just being in that person's presence.

If you are sensitive to this human need for quiet companionship, you know when to speak and when to simply enjoy silence together. Maybe it's how God made us. And maybe that's because he is that way too.

Our Lord does speak in words—through the Bible and through his own Son. Jesus. He even sends an angel down to mortals, now and again, with messages of importance. But God also knows the value of silence. And that, if you listen closely, is what you might learn from a starlit sky.

The Holy Spirit, says the apostle Paul, is there to help you in your weakness, when you do not know how to pray.

He intercedes for you with groanings that are too deep for words. Let your ears have a rest, and listen with your heart instead. Hear the love that reverberates within every shimmering star. Take that love times ten billion and you may have a tiny inkling of your Creator's tender thoughts toward you.

Since the creation of the world God's invisible qualities — his eternal power and divine nature — have been clearly seen, being understood from what has been made.
ROMANS 1:20

Our safest eloquence concerning him is our silence, when we confess without confession that his glory is inexplicable, his greatness above our capacity and reach.
RICHARD HOOKER

Dear Lord:

Thank you for allowing me to be silent in your presence, simply soaking up the love and peace and joy you provide. I receive it as one lost in and satisfied by your goodness and mercy.

Amen.

Riding the Waves of Glory

Behold, I am coming soon! My reward is with me, and I will give to everyone according to what he has done.

REVELATION 22:12

You buckle your life jacket and hop into the raft. Your adrenaline is pumping. You take hold of the oar and do as you're instructed. Although the river looks calm, and you're with the best tour guide in the area, you know you're about to take the plunge of your life. As you drift downstream, the current picks up. The raging rapids come into view. Up and down you bounce with the waves, the water splashes your face, soaks your body, and threatens to take you under. But you keep paddling, until, once again, you're safe and sound on that peaceful river.

A raging river can be a real challenge. Experienced tour guides pay attention to weather patterns so they can lead their groups through at just the right time. The world you live in is raging also. Wars and suffering are everywhere. Hurricanes, earthquakes, natural disasters abound. The Bible says that the world will be in this state of turmoil when Jesus returns to put evil to rest, and you are to watch for the signs —just as the tour guides watch the weather. In this way, you are to prepare for his coming—a most wonderful event for those who have placed their trust in him.

If you are watchful and expectant, you need not fear the raging rapids. Even though you may have to deal with a powerful current and you may end up soaked through to the skin, he will see that you make it through. You may even go through with great excitement, knowing that when the rapids subside you will find yourself basking in the peaceful presence of your mighty Savior and God.

The Lord himself will come down from heaven,
with a loud command, with the voice of the
archangel and with the trumpet call of God, and
the dead in Christ will rise first. After that, we
who are still alive and are left will be caught up
together with them in the clouds to meet the Lord
in the air. And so we will be with the Lord
forever.
1 THESSALONIANS 4:16-17

The only way to wait for the Second Coming is
to watch that you do what you should do, so
when he comes is a matter of indifference.
OSWALD CHAMBERS

Dear Lord:

How wonderful that day will be when you come to reign and rule
on this earth — the promised Messiah in all your power and glory.
Until that day, I will watch the signs so that when you come, I will
be ready and waiting.

Amen.

Rooted and Grounded in Christ

Like newborn babies, crave pure spiritual milk,
so that by it you may grow up in your salvation.
1 PETER 2:2

The grass around your cabin is green, lush, and alive. It feels soft under your bare feet. How does it flourish so with no human hand to tend it? There are many natural nutrients that affect the growth of grass, as well as the texture, and even how it looks. Rainwater, sun, and good, rich soil are just a few. Runoff from the snowpack provides moisture, even during dry conditions; trees and bushes along the hillside provide stability for the soil, and the sun has full play at so high an altitude.

Your spiritual life can be as full and vibrant and amazing as the grass outside your cabin door—even more because your heart is not subject to the uncertainty the natural environment must endure. The brush fire that eliminates the bushes on the hillside may allow for a mudslide. The early high temperatures that melt the snowpack too quickly may cause flooding. These are perils for the grass under your feet, but not for the faith in your heart. As long as you are doing your part, God is faithful to guard your heart against adverse conditions.

As you take in the nutrients in the soul of God's Word by reading and studying daily, you will be well on your way to a healthy and thriving spiritual life. Next you must keep the moisture level high by spending time in God's presence praying and praising him. When we do this we are partaking of living water. We should also preserve our spiritual life by spending time in the sunshine of Christian fellowship and encouragement. When you are doing these things, you can be assured that you will be growing lush and green, filled with vibrant spiritual life.

You must make every effort to support your faith with goodness. and goodness with knowledge, and knowledge with self-control, and self-control with endurance, and endurance with godliness, and godliness with mutual affection, and mutual affection with love.
2 PETER 1:5-7 NRSV

The strongest principle of growth lies in human choice.
GEORGE ELIOT

Dear Lord:

Thank you for the living water that flows from your presence. Thank you for spiritual nutrients present in your Word. And thank you for the sunshine of encouragement that comes from my fellow believers. May I grow stronger and more alive with every passing day.

Amen.

Cycle of Life

---

*[Jesus said.] "The words I have spoken to you are
spirit and they are life."*
J O H N   6 : 6 3

Y ou sit at the river's edge and watch the salmon. They're amazing fish. Instead of going with the current, they swim against it, upstream. As they flip and flop over and above each wave you're mesmerized by their determination, strength, and power. Yet, you know, their final end is certain. They will eventually reach that safe harbor, lay their eggs, and die.

This would seem to be the way of human life as well. Struggle and more struggle only to arrive at the destination in time to die. The plight of the salmon does indeed illustrate the futility of life without God, but it does not speak for those who place their trust in him.

As God's child, you can expect to encounter difficulties on your journey through life. You may often feel that you are swimming upstream, against the philosophies of this world. You may experience rapids that throw you back and forth and can even flip you out of the water and onto the shore. You may think that your journey, your struggle, will never end, but God will see to it you reach your destination.

And when you reach that place, that very special place you have been swimming toward all your life, you will find much more than death. You will find newness of life, rest from your journey, and the eternal presence of God. Your struggles, unlike the salmon's, will result in everlasting life.

Your life could be like the salmon's—full of struggle and without hope. But God has given you more—much more.

> *Jesus said to her, "I am the resurrection and the*
> *life. He who believes in me will live, even though*
> *he dies; and whoever lives and believes in me will*
> *never die. Do you believe this?"*
> JOHN 44:25-26

> *Your suffering, your struggles are never wasted*
> *in God. They are certainly one of the currencies*
> *of heaven.*
> ANDREA GARNEY

Dear Lord:

I want to make my journey, following you wherever you want me
to go. Though I may encounter struggles, I know you will be there
to help me push through to victory, until I finally arrive at my
destination and receive the crown of life you have prepared for me.

Amen.

True Contentment

I know the best thing we can do is to always enjoy life,
because God's gift to us is the happiness we get from
our food and drink and from the work we do.
ECCLESIASTES 3: 12-13 CEV

As night closes in, you step onto the deck, of your cabin and gaze at the brilliant sliver of moon. Darkness surrounds you. Stars, like shimmering crystals, light up the sky. A cool breeze flowing down from the mountain kisses your hair and skin. The world once again is peaceful and quiet — content.

What a contrast to things back home — everyone pushing for bigger, better, and more. But as you examine the vast canopy above your head, you realize a simple truth: real beauty, real value, real life is often covered up by the city lights. The never-ending advertisements urging you to buy this and eat that. The constant pressure to be like those around you, to provide for your children the things others are providing. The push to achieve more, make more, gain a higher position. These are all loud and unnaturally bright, keeping your eyes from seeing the stars sparkling directly overhead.

Fortunately, this place has given you the opportunity to consider what you really have, what you really want, who you really are. It has succeeded in screening out the noise and the distractions so that you can see clearly.

You will never be happy chasing after the things of this world. God has placed a desire for eternal things in your heart and it will always be there deep inside, waiting to be discovered when the distractions have been removed. As you leave this wonderful place and travel back to your home in the city, don't forget the lesson you learned tonight. The temporary, materialistic things of this world are only amusements. They cannot bring you true and lasting happiness. They cannot bring you contentment. Only God can do that.

I have learned to be content with whatever I have. I know what it is to have little, and I know what it is to have plenty. In any and all circumstances I have learned the secret of being well-fed and of going hungry, of having plenty and of being in need.
PHILIPPIANS 4:11 – 12 NRSV

It is so important not to waste what is precious by spending all one's time and emotion on fretting or complaining over what one does not have.
EDITH SCHAEFFER

Heavenly Father:

Even here as I close my eyes in prayer, I can see the precious things you have provided for me – love, courage, peace, family, friends, and most of all, personal relationship with you. When the things of this world begin to press in on me, demanding my attention, give me a nudge and I'll return to this quiet place where I know the meaning of contentment.

Amen.

Pushing Through the Fog

*Whoever listens to me will live in safety and be
at ease, without fear of harm.*

P R O V E R B S   1 : 3

As you drive cautiously along the narrow, winding, mountain road, a thick, dense fog closes in on the mountains around you. You can only see a car length ahead. Part of you is saying maybe it's best to head back. You even consider stopping to find a room for the night, yet you are anxious to get back to your mountain retreat. What to do?

Just as it's tough to make the call whether to continue on in the fog, it's also sometimes difficult to discern things in your spiritual life. There are so many good things you could do. so many directions you could take, so many talents you have to share. Yet if you don't have strong direction, you could veer off the road and end up never fulfilling the destiny the Lord has for you.

Fortunately, God has given you a fog buster to keep your spiritual life on track. It's his Word — the Bible. He says it's a light for your path and lantern for your feet. Reading, studying, and spending time in the Word will give you that understanding you need to make good choices for your life, to reach your destiny, to accomplish God's will. Coupled with the still, small voice of the Holy Spirit inside you. the timeless truths of the Bible will illuminate the road ahead, giving you just the clarity you need.

You may have to inch through the fog to arrive at your cabin hideaway, but you will never have to be in the fog about God's will for your life. If you're looking, he will show you the way.

Preserve sound judgment and discernment, do not let them out of your sight; they will be life for you, an ornament to grace your neck. Then you will go on your way in safety, and your foot will not stumble; when you lie down, you will not be afraid; when you lie down, your sleep will be sweet.
P R O V E R B S 3 : 2 1 - 2 4

I said to the man who stood at the gate of the year: "Give me a light that I may tread safely into the unknown." And he replied: "Go out into the darkness and put your hand into the hand of God. That shall be to you better than light, and safer than a known way."
M I N N I E L . H A S K I N S

Heavenly Father:

I feel like I'm in a fog sometimes, barely able to make out the road ahead. You are always there, though, always close at hand, leading and guiding me, making sure I arrive safely. Thank you for the light you bring to my life.

Amen.

Standing Firm as the Mountains

The steadfast love of the Lord never ceases, his mercies never come to an end; they are new every morning; great is your faithfulness.
LAMENTATIONS 3:22-23 NRSV

Mountains and promises . . . you ponder the connection. Examples from the Bible immediately flood your memory:

It was on the side of a mountain, after the Great Flood, that the ark landed, holding all remaining life—the seed of the future God promised through his rainbow. Moses met with God on a mountaintop to receive the Ten Commandments, God's covenant with his people. It was on a hillside that Jesus delivered his most famous oratory, the Sermon on the Mount, in which he promised blessing after blessing to those who would follow his ways.

God intended his promises to stand. Though we are fickle and faithless, he remains true to his everlasting covenant. He must have had good reason for choosing mountains to communicate his character. He must have known how well they would represent his unfailing, unchanging nature.

You have explored these mountains, hiked their trails, taken on the challenge of scaling their steep inclines, slept beneath the stars hovering over them. You've gained a healthy respect for their dangers and grown to trust their solidness. You readily understand, now, some truths about God that he had hidden for you in these stately, rugged places.

You read his promises here, in the tranquility. You believe them more firmly than ever, and you accept the challenge of walking in them, however steep the way. Christ is your solid rock, steadfast and immovable. Open your mouth and thank him for teaching you the lessons of these mountains — lessons that will go with you as you return to life as usual, lessons that will now be strong within you for the remainder of your days.

You know with all your heart and soul that not one of all the good promises the Lord your God gave you has failed. Every promise has been fulfilled; not one has failed.
JOSHUA 23:14

God's promises are like the stars; the darker the night the brighter they shine.
DAVID NICHOLAS

Heavenly Father:

Your promises are so precious to me. Of course they are! For they represent everything that is good and important and permanent in my life. They even provide hope of life after death. Best of all, they are backed by the very power of your Word — the Word that created everything I see before me.

Amen.

Additional copies of this and other products
from Honor Books are available online and
at your local bookseller.

———————————————————

Also available from Honor Books:

Beach Prayers: A Vacation for Your Soul